PRAISE FOR LISA

"Lisa is beautiful inside and out. She consta... g ... and will inspire anyone who reads the book."

—Kathy Coover
Co-founder and Executive Vice President, Isagenix

"When Hurricane Sandy hit the Jersey shore, Lisa opened up her home and her heart to her friends and some team members. She's a giving, caring, super-smart leader who helps her team and herself through any adversity. Lisa is always smiling and laughing, finding joy in the trying times of life. We can all learn from her."

—Dr. Paul Anderson M.D., D.A.A.P.M.
CEO of Natural Health

"Lisa is a true marketing expert and leader. She motivates women to be the best in every aspect of our lives—to support other women, be great moms, be fabulous partners at home, and be true leaders in our careers. Lisa gives you the tools and makes you find the confidence within yourself to conquer the world. I highly recommend this book and hope both women and men of all ages give themselves the gift of the book, which will only enhance their lives."

—Lisa Ben-Isvy
Associate Publisher *Promenade* Magazine and
Associate Publisher, *New York Metro Parents*

"Lisa DeMayo is a dear friend and a beautiful person who truly exemplifies the real meaning of 'making a difference by being the difference.' I am so excited about her new book, The Art of Getting What You Want—a book I am sure will inspire and motivate many to seek their greatest potential, achieve great success, and change lives."

—Ed Natera
Serial Entrepreneur

"I consider Lisa DeMayo to be one of America's most influential entrepreneurs. Her book is a winner. Buy it now."

—Dr. Tony O'Donnell
Naturopath & Author

THE ART

of

GETTING WHAT YOU WANT

THE ART
of
GETTING WHAT YOU WANT

How to Cultivate the Happiness, Health,

and Wealth You Desire

LISA DEMAYO

DUNHAM
books

Dunham Books
63 Music Square East
Nashville, Tennessee 37203
www.dunhamgroupinc.com

Trade paperback ISBN: 978-1-939447-81-4
Ebook ISBN: 978-1-939447-82-1

Printed in the United States of America

To all those who believe they can. And, especially to my three children—Gianna, Victoria and Nicky—you will forever be my reason, never my excuse. I love you unconditionally.

TABLE OF CONTENTS

FOREWORD

This is the moment to acknowledge that you are the owner of your own life. You are not a bystander or an eyewitness. You are in the thick of it. You and you alone own your moments. The question is: what are you going to do with them?

Have you ever read the book *Love Does* by Bob Goff? Bob is an attorney. But he's so much more than an attorney. He's a man who lives his life in such a way that most of us would if we could only just shed ourselves of our self-defeating inhibitions and cumbersome expectations. Bob says, "Something happens when you feel ownership. You no longer act like a spectator or consumer—because you're an owner."

Wise, wise man.

A Los Angeles resident, Bob claims his office is at Disneyland on Tom Sawyer's Island. He says he does all his best thinking there at the "picnic table at the end of a little pier right across from the pirate ship."

At first blush, this, of course, sounds ridiculous. No sane-brained fellow—especially no attorney—would take up office space in the land of adventure, folly, and toddlers. But Bob Goff actually does. Because being magical, because being allowed to dream and do the unthinkable, is very worthwhile. And he realizes that magic is so much more valuable than cubicle space in life.

Bob writes, "Here's a strange truth I've noticed. Almost everyone knows about Tom Sawyer Island at Disneyland, but most people don't go. Maybe it's because it's surrounded by water and you have to take a raft to get there. But it's really not that tough to do. Lots of people want to go. Some people even plan to go. But most forget, or just don't get around to it. It's one of those 'we'll do that next trip' kinds of places for a lot of people. Tom Sawyer Island is like most people's lives I think: they never get around to crossing over to it."

Living a life fully engaged and full of whimsy and love is something most people plan to do, but along the way they just kind of forget. Their dreams become one of those "we'll go there next time" deferrals. The sad thing is, for many there is no "next time" because passing on the chance to cross over is an overall attitude toward life rather than a single decision. Most people think they need more opportunities, but what they really need is a change of attitude.

As I write this, I am now sixty-eight years old. I've spent the bulk of my life dedicated to helping others maximize their potential and live their dream life. This starts by helping people change their attitudes, which ultimately does provide them with more opportunities. And the most important part of maximizing your potential is taking ownership of your life.

Not tomorrow.

Not next week.

But today.

Right now.

Maximizing your potential is about not deferring your hopes and dreams, ultimately missing out—like so many do with Tom Sawyer Island at Disneyland—but instead taking advantage of every opportunity, allowing yourself to believe that your world is bigger than what you're currently settling for.

I have been a long-time fan of Lisa DeMayo. She has a spirit that is absolutely contagious. And I'm so thrilled she's finally put it all down on paper for us. I believe the wisdom found in this book will rub right off onto you. In these pages, Lisa tells stories—many deeply personal—that really display the art of true-life ownership. She sets down in words not just a few good ideas, but genuine roadmaps to getting what you've always desired out of life.

Lisa does not believe in the art of quick fixes or hidden secrets that will unveil a new life in 30 seconds flat. She wants much more for your life than a momentary about-face. She wants real change. Lifelong change. Much like I do, Lisa believes in the power of the individual and the power of attitude changes.

I hope you will read this book eagerly. I hope you will soak up its wisdom and then choose to take action and really own your life. Your past is in your past, but it's up to you how you author your future.

Shall we begin?

—Jack Canfield

PREFACE

Life is a journey, not a destination. Do you believe that? I do. And do you know why? Because the final destination, like it or not, is death. Not one of us is exempt from getting out of the game of life alive. Everything eventually will be gone—our fears, dreams, hopes, humiliations, excitement—all of it. All each of us leaves behind is a legacy and some memories to be shared amongst friends and family for a few generations.

That can be a hard pill to swallow, I know. But the sooner you believe this—the sooner you start living for the journey and not the destination and the sooner you'll really have a chance at having the life you desire.

I've seen too many good people fooled by promises of better tomorrows. The day-to-day is where it's happening. Right now. This very second. Last I checked, tomorrow wasn't a guarantee for any of us, so we may as well do what we love today. It could be our only chance. And there's so much freedom in that—in diving into this present second and not postponing the life we want. Forget the past, too. Don't get bogged down by your regrets and mistakes. They happened; they're over. Instead, choose to live this day to the max. Laugh, love, play, work, and give generously. Isn't that so much more worthwhile than pining after a time you can't get back to?

I believe my future is a clean slate. Do you? If so, are you living like you believe it? If not, when will you start?

And that's the first question you really must ask yourself. *Will today be the day you start living for the life you want?* And only if you're prepared to answer with an unqualified yes—no if's or maybes or dependings thrown into the mix—should you really move forward with reading this book. Because this book is about changing your life radically. And you can't experience the joy of radical life change if you're towing the line. Trying just won't do.

Making the quality of your life better—whether that be emotionally, physically, relationally, professionally, or financially—is an "all in" kind of endeavor. You're either here to be better, or you've resigned yourself to one of two fates: staying the same or tumbling downhill.

What will it be?

Projections and Possibilities

The first way to assess where you are is to ask yourself an honest question: do I believe in *possibilities* or is *impossible* my immediate response? The answer to that simple question will give you so much insight into where you stand.

We live in a society of dreamers. Most people want to believe that the life they *can* have is so much bigger than the life they *do* have. Deep inside them, most people feel—and are right to feel—that they're born with a giant capacity for greatness. They have talents and gifts that were meant to be utilized. They have ideas and plans that deserve to come to fruition. The problem is so many dreamers stop there. At dreaming. And they let those dreams get tackled by thoughts of impossibility and failure.

As humans, we have this unfortunate tendency to get cloaked in doubt. Our biggest hopes and ideas get overtaken by things like daily habit and societal expectations. We get stuck in automatic and forget that our life is full of choices and those choices are what shape us. There are, in fact, very few things that anyone has to do. We don't all have to go off the same template. Our life doesn't have to look this way. We're allowed to deviate. We were *created* to deviate. So why aren't we allowing ourselves to pursue the life we feel called to? Why are we lying to ourselves about our options?

How many of you speak in such a way that your own opinions have become an absolute truth for you? What I mean by that is: do you put more stock in your assessment of your life or in actual reality? We can all choose to look at the same situation differently. But over time, we become so automatic in our response that we truly believe what we say about our life, even if it isn't true.

Here's an example. There are some absolute truths or assertions: I am a woman. I have three children: Gianna, Victoria, and Nick. That's true about me. An interpretation is that I have the best luck, no luck, no time, too busy, the best friends, no support, and on it goes. It depends on how I see the situation. But these interpretations, if I tell them to myself often enough, can start to look less like opinions and more like truths. And that's a dangerous situation if my opinions are filled with doubt.

Our capacity for a greater journey and more fulfilled life is the result of change. Change your words, change your thoughts, change your actions, and get different results.

In order to have the life you want, you have to shift what you believe about yourself.

Some of you will put the book down here. You would rather be right about the story you've made up about your life and circumstance than get a little uncomfortable and shake things up. Well, humor me for a second and try this on for size before you throw in the towel on the good life.

Our lives are mostly based on our interpretations of our past and a *projected* future. If the future isn't looking so good right now, chances are you have low energy, fear, and are disconnected. But if the future looks good, you have abundant energy, a sunny disposition, and a good attitude.

It is not truth or fact that is holding you back from a great future. It's your *fears* and your *projections* of what could go wrong that hold you back. If you change your projections and create a good story that moves you forward, your future can be bright and full and fulfilled. But you have to believe in it. You have to start telling yourself the right story.

What Gets in the Way of the Right Story

So what gets in the way of telling the right story? Put simply: our fear. Most of us want to believe in fairytale endings. But then, because we're human, we harken to worst-case scenarios. The potential in front of us becomes overshadowed by the pitfalls of change.

We get scared.

We cringe.

We begin measuring ourselves up with everyone else.

We look at the obstacles in the way and begin to reason that our lives aren't really that bad after all. And when we do that, when we start to justify and explain away our hopes, when we're willing to settle, it's all downhill. *Is the dream worth it?* We ask ourselves. *Is the dream even possible?* As a result, the dream doesn't ever become anything. Instead, it remains what it began as: a crazy idea. A wish.

We've told ourselves the wrong story.

If you really think about it, most people don't lack dreams; they lack conviction. They don't live their lives with a clear understanding of who they are, what they want, and what they're capable of, ultimately leading to half-hearted existences. In other words, they go through their days without certainty and intention. And without certainty and intention, nothing big is possible. Instead of living an incredible life, we decide it's enough to just get by.

I wrote *The Art of Getting What You Want* because I know that hoping is not enough. The blessings I've experienced and the life I'm fortunate to lead is not a result of a wealthy upbringing. I didn't have anything handed to me. I was not "lucky" or in a position of favor. Instead, I was a decision-maker. I was a perseverer. I chose to be a person of certainty rather than a person of doubt. I chose to tell myself a positive story.

I use commitments as my resources. You have to give your word and follow through with what you say you're going to do. Create actions from your commitments not your circumstance. What is really important to you? Commit to doing actions necessary to have that. Too often we act from a place of what *should* be important to us rather than what *is* important to us. When we only do what others expect, we're left empty and unfilled. But when we do what's important to us, when we're willing to tell ourselves a story of success and fulfillment, the end result can be beautiful.

In *Think and Grow Rich*, Napoleon Hill introduces us to Edwin C. Barnes, a man who was absolutely determined to partner with the great inventor Thomas Edison. It was a ridiculous notion to most, but to Barnes it was the only possible future. So he travelled from the Midwest to West Orange, New Jersey by train on this simple, but determined hope, and inevitably he achieved his goal. In fact, the Barnes/Edison partnership is one of the greatest business stories in history. Napoleon Hill writes, "Maybe young Barnes did not know it at the time, but his bulldog determination, his persistence in standing back of a single Desire, was destined to mow down all opposition, and bring him the opportunity he was seeking."

I imagine you've been told a great deal about what success looks like and the path you need to take to get there. I bet there's a laundry list of degrees and experiences you're expected to get before you can have the life you want. But I also bet you're reading this right now because something about the whole process—something about this standard formula—is just plain unsatisfying. All of this expecting hasn't given you much of what you expected at all. Instead, it's left you rather disappointed. You've spent so much time trying to be what everyone says you need to be that who you are, and I mean who you *really* are, has been pushed to the wayside.

This is your one and only life. Do you only want what other people expect for you? Or do you want more? Are you willing to be like Barnes and charge forward despite the doubters? Do you want to start exceeding all of your wildest expectations?

If so, it's time to start telling yourself the right story.

CHAPTER 1
Go Manual

"A life spent making mistakes is not only more honorable, but more useful than a life spent doing nothing."

—George Bernard Shaw

It will be a good time to start. Soon. Not now, of course. That's too soon. There's too much that has to be done between now and then.

Before then, before I really start, I need to have more money. I need to be out of debt. The kids need to be out of school. I need to find a partner. I need to lose weight. I need to get my life in order. My spouse needs to get a promotion. I need to have a solid business plan. I need to build a safety net. The ducks must be in their proper rows. I need to get that Master's degree. And I need to have no doubts. This, beyond all else, has to be a sure thing.

Sound familiar?

Is there one more item you must check off your list before you finally do what you say you've wanted to do for months, even years? And does the list somehow keep getting longer and longer, forever postponing this dream future you fantasize about?

If this is the case, you are drowning in fear of failure. Your life is being directed far more by worst-case scenario than best-case scenario.

Oh wait! You say. *That's not me! I always go for the risk!* And maybe you do.

Even if things aren't lined up perfectly, you dive in headfirst. But still, there's something about your life that doesn't feel complete. Your soul is searching for something more. Do you ever feel that way? Trust me, I so get all of it. Life is a journey of knowing and continuing to grow. You just have to get rid of all the junk in the way to see clearly.

In so many ways, the route to success is about elimination. By the time you turn the final page of this book, my hope for you is that you will have discarded the unnecessary chaos and baggage you've been lugging around. A layer of skin will be peeled off. And it will feel so good to be walking around lighter and more clear-headed.

But in order to get to that point, you have to start. You have to stop making excuses and allowing for delays. You have to stop caking on roadblocks. You have to take your life off automatic and begin directing the course of your days manually, making decisions and choices that intentionally lead you to the life you want.

It sounds so simple and obvious, doesn't it? But you'd be surprised. The majority of aspirers get caught in the land of wishing. They mull, and brood, and dream. But they never really get the gumption to dive in and begin.

So let's start now. Here. With this book. Commit to reading it end-to-end. Commit to actively changing your attitude, perspective, and actions. It starts now, or it doesn't start at all.

Worthiness

So let's start by asking yourself an important question: Are you good enough? And I mean really ask yourself that. Do you truly believe you're good enough to have the life you dream of? Do you think you're talented enough? Smart enough? *Worthy enough?*

It's a hard question to ask if you're willing to be honest. The kneejerk reaction is, "Yes, of course. I'm absolutely good enough." But chances are, that's a defensive yes. Not an honest yes.

Most of us will find when we really stop and evaluate our lives, our actions and decisions don't reflect a confidence in our abilities and potential. Instead, they reinforce the "safe" lives we're comfortable with and know we can handle. As a result, our daily decisions limit our futures rather than help us realize our dreams.

This book is all about helping you achieve the life you want by changing your decision-making patterns and personal belief systems. And that starts, first and foremost, with believing you're worthy. I know this because for so long I didn't see myself as worthy. I had a small-minded view of who I was and, in turn, I was capsizing my ability to succeed.

I grew up in Queens just outside the city. I was the third of four children, born to a mother without a high school education and a father who never made it to college. My childhood, though, was pretty great. Sweet in that innocent way. I had good friends and just enjoyed the small pleasures. When you're young, you don't really understand if you're poor or wealthy as long as you have love. And while my parents struggled to put food on the table, they did care immensely. I was a daddy's girl, and all the bad in life that would show its hand later was cloaked by childhood imagination and fervor. I thought I had it good, and so I did.

When I hit high school, reality came rushing through the door. I transferred schools and had to take two buses to get there. It was an all girls school. I realized then that I didn't have money. While other girls were flaunting new clothes and fancy items, I was wearing the same outfit day after day. I drove a beat-up Dodge Dart with no air-conditioning, heat, or working windows. I bought the car myself for $500. I should have felt proud, but I hated it because it wasn't what I wanted for my life. I knew, at this time, my "ride" would forever be different.

Then there was the drugs and alcohol. I know more about either than I care to admit. I was surrounded by them growing up. They were everywhere and life, it seemed, was always a test. I watched the spirit that makes you "become somebody" die within those I dearly loved.

But despite all this, and maybe because of it, I knew what I wanted for my life and I knew it wasn't what I had. I was determined, from even the youngest age, to change my reality.

A large part of my believing spirit came from my dad. He always told me I was different. That I'd be something amazing, something we couldn't even dream up because it was so big. I'd fantasize about becoming a celebrity, living in California and buying a ranch so my dad could take care of the horses. The hairbrush became my microphone as I practiced public speaking in the mirror for years. In my head I had already arrived.

The year I turned thirteen though, the ground underneath me shifted. My dad was diagnosed with brain and lung cancer. We all tried to go about our normal lives, making meals, going to school, playing with friends, but all the while he was dying in the middle of the living room. There was a chemo drip and round-the-clock nurses. Everything in the house was dampened by his spirit. You could just see it fading away into the midst of cushions, lamps, and rugs. I did the best I could to take care of him, spoiling him, but it takes your breath away to lose someone that important to you.

Senior year, he passed. I spent my eighteenth birthday staring at him in a coffin. Two weeks later I graduated. The funny thing was, I never shared about his sickness with any of my friends or teachers at school. They all assumed my absences were from a lack of caring. My friends at home became—and remain—my rock.

Things were bubbling inside me then. Feelings. Secrets. Uncertainty about who I was and who I'd become. *Questions about my worthiness.* I was always a skinny little thing growing up, but when my dad got sick and I started eating with him, I saw my body change in ways I didn't like. I became consumed with my appearance. I spiraled down into a depression and tried to control it. I was quiet about my struggle and kept it a secret from everyone, burying it deep inside. No one knew, and I didn't understand how devastating my choices were to myself, both mentally and physically.

And so in the thick of high school, while my dad was dying and my brothers and sister were battling their own demons, I was just drowning in this poor self-image, living a lie. One morning, I woke up and was too weak to get out of bed. I remember lying there, wishing I would die and thinking about how I could do it. But then I thought about my Mom who I love so very much. She had been devastated by all that was going on, and she didn't deserve any more heartache. So that day I made a hard decision and I chose. I chose to let go and surrender to the fact that I needed help. I chose to undergo a very long, spiritual and personal-development journey. And I chose to believe it would be worth it.

You will hear about my mentor, Robin, a few chapters in, but as I began my coaching career she would often say to people, "Don't let her looks fool you; she is wise beyond her years. Because of what she's endured, she can listen to almost all of you without judgment." And man, is that true. No matter what people tell me, it's okay. How can I judge you? I was a train wreck!

Eventually my heart was filled not only with compassion, but also with acceptance about who I am and where I came from. I tried to believe. I focused all my energy on personal development. I got my hands on as much positive thinking material as I could find. I'd listen to tapes on repeat. I took coaching workshops and courses. I began to understand the importance of self-reliance, self-confidence, and self-awareness. At the heart of it, I knew I had to change the underlying conversation in my life. I had to find my sea legs and believe in my self-worth. For so long I had told myself I wasn't good enough. The grace I was so willing and eager to extend to others in my life, I couldn't offer myself. But I knew if I wanted to move forward, I'd have to eat a big piece of that humble pie and not worry about judgment. *Who cares what other people think of you*, I would tell myself. *The important thing is what you think of you.*

I started seeking out mentors, trying to etch my own path forward. Even though my family didn't have a long history of education, I put myself through college and graduated with a four-year degree. Because I was able to change my internal dialogue, I was able to change my future. It was a long, intentional journey and I had to choose to take it every day, but it was incredibly worth it.

Because of my experiences, I went on to a number of successful careers. I've been a top-performing pharmaceutical sales representative, a motivational life coach, a record-breaking sales consultant for two network marketing companies, a sought after business trainer, and a self-made millionaire. But my biggest accomplishment: three amazing children! And a body that I now respect and even like! How cool is that?

But yet no matter how great my life is, I always consider it a work in progress. There isn't a point where I'm "done." There have been times in my career where I began to coast—where I was making more money than I'd ever imagined and had a cushy situation, but I knew I wasn't moving forward. I wasn't growing. And because I didn't feel full, I knew I couldn't stay there. So each time I found myself hitting that plateau, I'd ask the hard question: is this the best you can do? And when the answer was inevitably no, I'd then have to ask myself: what are you willing to let go of to have what you don't have? Often the answer was comfort and security.

More than once, I walked away from six-figure salary jobs because I knew I'd plateaued there. It was scary to leave. It's always scary doing something different. But the really great things in life rarely come without asking you to be a little brave in the process.

My most recent hardship was ending a marriage of twelve years to an incredible man and the father of my three children. I love him, but we weren't "in love." When the conversation is, "It's not that bad," it's time to rethink. We both know that our kids are our reason, not our excuse, to separate. They deserve to see their parents as the best they can be, empowered by choice. I strongly believe no one should ever feel stuck.

I wrote this book for people like me who didn't start life with the perfect platform. Who didn't come into the world with a sizeable dowry and a basketful of contacts and a self-confidence that soared through the ceiling. No, instead I wrote this for the people who are willing to believe, no matter where they started and no matter where they are now, that success can be a sweet and sure certainty if you're only willing to take your life off automatic and become empowered by choice.

If someone today gave me the choice of being born into the world with a million dollars or a brave heart, every day of the week and twice on Sunday I'd choose heart. There's so much value in the soul who dares to be bold. And so I challenge you now as you move forward in this book, lean so far into the fear that you come out the other side a brighter and more courageous soul than ever before. It's time to start. And it's time to start now.

CHAPTER 2
Expand Your Worldview

"Deep within man dwell those slumbering powers; powers that would astonish him, that he never dreamed of possessing; forces that would revolutionize his life if aroused and put into action."

—Orison Swett Marden

Let's start with today. Just today. From the moment you wake up, there are many possible roads you can travel until you crawl back into bed at night. Most people view their days with few choices. Get up. Brew the coffee. Go to work. Drive home. Make dinner. They see their options as inconsequential. The outcomes are all the same no matter what they do. But that couldn't be farther from the truth.

Each day is filled with multiple choice points. These choice points are forks in the road where you can go left or right. They are the decisions that carve the route you're taking throughout your waking hours.

Are you going to go into work or are you going to call in sick? Are you going to meet your deadline or are you going to procrastinate? Are you going to use your free time to work on your passion project or are you going to spend it catching up on the reality TV shows you taped? Are you going to work on your relationship with your boss or are you going to continue resenting him?

It is the decisions you make—even in the small things—that crucially determine the course of your life. You can go through the day typically. You can nod your head, you can shuffle your feet along, you can grumble and complain about the little things. But isn't there a better way?

After all, the history of our world is composed of big decisions made in seemingly small, average moments. There is no place too small to do a big thing. You never know in life when the average can become exceptional. It's high time you expand your worldview.

The Power of Interpretation

Most of potential is seized when people begin to realize the power of interpretation. The same event can happen and, depending on how you interpret it, you will be led down different roads.

One road may lead to sadness, boredom, or a lack of fulfillment. The other may lead to success, health, and happiness. The good news is what road you travel is up to you.

Here's an example of what I'm talking about. You know the organization Mothers Against Drunk Driving (MADD)? It was founded by women who had experienced the loss of the most precious thing in their lives, their children.

Beckie Brown, for instance, became an instrumental part of the organization when her son, Marcus Daniel Brown, died at age eighteen as a result of being involved in a car crash involving a nineteen-year-old drunk driver.

No one would have blamed Beckie if she closed the shutters and climbed into bed, turning off the lights. No one would have thought ill of her if she chose to weep, stay in, and be bitter about what happened, wondering always, "Why me?" People would have said that was understandable. What a horrific tragedy she endured. How could she possibly go on?

But Beckie knew that moment in her life was a choice point. She could go one of two ways. She could be bitter and continue the downward spiral, or she could channel her grief into something positive for others. Beckie chose the latter. She established the first MADD chapter in Northern Florida, helped organize Florida's statewide chapter, and was instrumental in passing numerous pieces of legislation on the state and national level. Inevitably, she served as MADD's national president.

Beckie decided to use her experience and her grief as a way to prevent this from happening to others in the future, as well as a way to help provide a support community for those who had endured the same heartbreak. She made a decision, and she chose the better road. It's all about how you interpret what has happened to you and how you choose to react.

When I think about the power of interpretation, I'm always reminded of Robinson Lynn. I've known Robinson since he was just a young boy, though he's now twenty-eight. His mom, Robin, was my mentor and dear, dear friend for many years. She founded the organization Momentum Education and spent her life investing in people and loving others. She was a powerhouse and my angel. She was the truth-talker when everyone else was too busy walking around on eggshells. You could always count on Robin to be "insignificant" enough to really help others because it was *never* about her. It was always about the person she was with and that person's worth. She wanted people to be the best version of themselves possible. Getting there wasn't always pretty, of course. Truth isn't the easiest pill to swallow, but it's always the best one. And Robin always gave her truth with a big heaping side of grace.

I saw this so many times in my life firsthand. Robin was brave enough to "get in my face" and "call me out," so that I would scoot out onto the skinny branch. I am where I am today in large part because this woman saw me as a leader and put her nose to my nose, and said straight to my face, "The world needs people like you, but you are so stingy and self absorbed that they won't get it from you."

It was a shocking thing to hear. But I knew what she meant. And I was thankful she had the guts to say it. If I wasn't willing to get on a skinny branch and get uncomfortable, I was being a fraction of the me I could be. I didn't hate her when she said it to me. No, I hated the small game that I'd been letting myself play. I'd bought into, "This is as good as it gets." But because Robin was willing to be honest, I soon remembered that good could get a lot greater.

When Robin's son, Robinson, was twenty-two years old, in October of 2009, Robin was diagnosed with pancreatic cancer.

Robinson then was a young man. He'd just graduated from college with a degree in American Studies. His parents had pooled together some money for his graduation and purchased him a round-the-world ticket. He was going to jet set off into the wild yonder, hopping from country to country.

But the cancer changed everything. The day she was diagnosed, a Tuesday I remember, she called and asked me to come over. I certainly wasn't prepared for what was going to happen. As I walked into her Upper East Side apartment, I had this sinking feeling in my stomach, and I knew she was dying.

It was one of the hardest times in my life. How could a woman who changed so many lives leave so soon? So prematurely?

I don't think any of us were prepared to continue her work. She was going to leave these massive shoes to fill. But always the supporter of others, Robin believed in us. And, most important, she believed in her son. He was born with and carries still her blood and her charisma and her deep sense of love for the people around her. While the rest of us might have bitten our nails and worried, Robin knew her legacy was going to continue and, while the cancer might take her life, it wasn't going to take that away from her.

The same week we found out about the cancer, her son— her twenty-two year old son with no business experience—was named acting director of her company. He was thrown into a world where he was leading and coaching people who were twice his age, all the while trying to process his mom's diagnosis, learn what he could from her, and spend time soaking her in. It was a whirlwind. And just three short months after that, Robin passed away. It seemed too quick and too painful for everyone, Robinson probably most.

"The first reaction I had to my mother's death," Robinson told me, "was pain. I couldn't stop thinking about how terrible it was. How unfair it seemed. But then I pulled myself back and realized there could be another interpretation. This second reaction I chose was gratitude. I had three months to say everything I wanted to say to my mother. I had three months to take care of her, nurture her, and say goodbye. And now I have this incredible opportunity to continue the amazing work she started. Not everyone has that. Even in the hardest situations, you can always choose a new interpretation. It's up to you to choose one that makes life better."

The great thing about Robinson's situation is that he was thrown haphazardly into his life's calling. He'd always spent a great deal of time with his mom and from a young age was prepared for a lifetime of service. In 1996, when he was ten, his mom plucked him up from the States and moved him to Cape Town, South Africa where they helped with the reconciliation process after the Apartheid. He spent Christmas day driving a freedom fighter to visit his incarcerated brother three hours away. His mom never posed their life of service as, "This is what we have to do," or "This is the right thing to do." Instead it was, "What a gift that we get to do this."

Robinson remembers being in college, interning at a PR company, unsure then of what he wanted to do with his life.

"I'd arrive at 9 a.m. and have to stay until 6 p.m.," he said. "I'd get there in the morning, check a few emails, get up and pace around the office and say hello, check my watch, go get a coffee, sit back at my desk, check my watch, go to the bathroom, go to the water cooler, check my watch again. And by then it was only 10:00 a.m. Time went so slow. But I remember that first week after my mom was diagnosed and I became acting director. We worked that day from 11:00 a.m. to 11:00 p.m., and I never checked my watch once. I was so engrossed in what we were doing. And that's how I knew this was my life's calling. Everyone should be doing something where you don't have to check your watch. How wonderful that my mom helped lead me to mine."

I watch Robinson now as he helps people choose to live powerful lives, where they realize the decision-making abilities they own, and how they can interpret their circumstances differently to create a better future. Like all of us who were blessed by his mom's gifts, Robinson knows it's *not* about him. It's about the people he's helping. It's about who he needs to be so the others around him can shift their paradigm and begin to live in a world that is much bigger and brighter and fruitful than they could ever have imagined.

He is his mother's son.

The Power of Resourcefulness

Hand-in-hand with the power of interpretation is the power of resourcefulness.

Chances are if you ask someone why they didn't achieve

something, they'll give you a laundry list of excuses. They'll say they didn't have the time, didn't have the money, didn't have the connections.

Sound familiar?

And while that's all well and good, and likely even true, the central element that determines your success is not the tools found in your arsenal, but rather the resourcefulness found in your mind and heart.

Are you familiar with the saying, "Burn the ships?" In the year 1519, Hernando Cortez, the Spanish conquistador, had sailed to the shores of Mexico. He traveled across the ocean with over 600 soldiers and sailors, and when his eleven ships landed in the Yucatan, they did so at the feet of a very large empire—the Aztecs.

The Aztecs, who had ruled their empire for six centuries, were an incredibly powerful and overwhelming foe. But instead of retreating and making the obvious decision—to leave—or even the second most obvious decision—to fight with the expectation of imminent loss—Cortez ordered his men to burn the ships.

Why? Because, as Cortez said, "If we're going home, we're going home in their ships." If he did not provide his men with a means to retreat, they had to succeed or die. The situation was incredibly clear, and his men moved forward with that conviction.

The Aztecs had all the tools and makings of a victor, but they did not have the resourcefulness or passion of Cortez and his Spanish troops. And so the mighty Aztecs were toppled all because a small group of men were willing to burn their ships.

Consider Robinson. When he took over his mom's business, he was only twenty-two. He was overwhelmed with the sudden terminal illness of a parent, had never had any business experience, and was thrown into a situation where he had to lead immediately. He didn't necessarily have the tools to succeed, but he had the guts to go for it. His wherewithal and resourcefulness, not his "experience," were what made all the difference.

Just as important, I have never once been in Robinson's presence and heard the "woe is me" song and dance you so often get from people who have lived through a tragedy. While Robinson has plenty to grieve about and a number of stories that would solicit tears and sympathy out of nearly every onlooker, he never plays the victim or the martyr. Robinson knows those titles would only burden him and limit his ability to be the man his mom so amazingly raised him to be. Instead, he chooses to access gratitude and acceptance, and this significant difference allows him to be a true leader.

If you want to have a full life, you must dig deep and look

always at what the alternatives are in any given situation. How many men quit just before they succeeded because they dared not look around the bend? Do not stop short because you're too small-minded about your capacity.

Give it all you've got. You'll find you've got far more than you ever expected.

Opening Your Mind

All of this—the power of interpretation, the power of resourcefulness—it's about something much bigger: expanding your worldview.

People are conditioned to believe that lives are supposed to be led a certain way. That society is the way that it is and there's little flexibility when it comes to changing the mold.

But when you buy into this, you're being guided more by your situation than your own personal doctrines. You're falling into the trap of believing that you are your past. But what's come before does not have to come after. You don't have to allow your past—or society's story—to become your story.

I've worked with tens of thousands of individuals over twenty years, and I've realized through every interaction that people can change their life instantaneously. Practically everything about who you are can be remodeled. But in order to change your life, you first and foremost must raise the stakes. As Henry

David Thoreau wrote, "I know of no more encouraging factor than the unquestionable ability of man to elevate his life by a conscious endeavor."

You must be aware first of your standards, then of your ability to change those standards. If you expect average, you will receive average. Only if you expect a higher standard of living, and consciously pursue it, will you be able to achieve one.

Ask yourself these questions:

1. Do you want to live a better life?

2. Do you feel like you're settling?

3. Are your resources—money, time, and connections—the only things holding you back?

4. Is the fear of failure driving your life rather than the potential of success?

If you answered yes to these questions, you can be assured that you're living too small. The good news is that you have the capacity to live bigger and better now. You can change your reality this instant.

First, you must believe it's possible. I can't help you if you're resistant to what I'm telling you, so don't waste anyone's time if you're not playing for keeps. You are where you are right now because of your *reaction* to your circumstance, not because of your circumstance. This book is filled with stories of people who have had to overcome significant obstacles to get where they are. They made a choice to overcome, as you must make a choice now. So choose. Stay where you are, or don't. It's really that simple.

If your "story" and your "situation" work for you, then keep doing what you're doing. But if even the slightest change will benefit you in some capacity, *choose* to create the change. The difference between those who do and those who don't is *choice*. Once you make the choice to have different results, you then can change your actions and your destiny.

You have the power.

Sound overwhelming? Don't get bogged down by the big picture. You just need to believe that you can create new action steps and then you need to choose to take those steps. Can you do that? I believe you can, but it's up to you to *choose* if it's worth it.

I want you to take out your journal and answer these questions thoughtfully. Don't rush through this exercise. You're taking a personal inventory of who you are and who you want to be. There is nothing more important than truly understanding yourself and raising the expectations you have for your life, so enjoy this time. Delve into it.

There is no better way you could spend your afternoon.

1. What controls and drives you on a daily basis? Is it fear? Is it unnecessary commitment? Is it safety?

2. How would your life look different if you chose to be driven by hope, potential, excitement, and passion rather than by negative factors, such as fear?

3. Consider the negative influences in your life that hold you back, whether they be habits (smoking, excessive drinking), people (naysayers), or commitments (9 to 5 jobs that keep you checking your watch). What will you no longer allow to be a part of your life? What decisions will you make to remove these unhealthy factors? Is it worth it to you to make the hard choice?

4. What goals would you pursue if resources (time, money, etc.) were not an issue?

5. List three ways you interpret your situation differently to begin pursuing your goals regardless of resources. In other words, how can you "burn your ships" so you can move full steam ahead?

CHAPTER 3
Your Own Glass Ceiling

"All truth passes through three stages. First, it is ridiculed. Second, it is violently opposed. Third, it is accepted as being self-evident."

—Arthur Schopenhauer

I have a friend, Rebecca. And she's not just a good friend, she's the best kind of friend. She's the type of individual where, when you spend time with her, you leave feeling like the good parts of you have swelled up and the bad parts of you have faded away. She's the friend you can't imagine not having in your life.

I met Rebecca when I was eighteen. I was working full time as a receptionist at an entertainment company, putting myself through college, and Rebecca was this powerful source of energy in the office. She was larger than life, full of purpose. I'd just lost my dad to cancer and was struggling to help support my mom, and she came along at just the right time. I had no idea how much she'd come to mean to me.

I remember early on being shocked at how Rebecca carried

herself. And it wasn't so much the attitude, really—even though her presence was remarkable. Rather, it was the timing. After all, when I met her it had only been a year since the accident.

When Rebecca was young, before I knew her, she was a dancer. She danced in the American Ballet Theater, trained at the Tisch School of Arts, at Carnegie Hall. Anywhere you could name. She had these long, graceful limbs that could turn and lift and lengthen with such poise and precision. It was startling really. Her delicacy. And she was beautiful, too. Young and fresh faced. Clear, glowing eyes that could see the future before her.

And Rebecca wanted a big future. Fame. She had plans for dancing and acting. Stardom. But when she was only twenty-years-old, she was out with some friends in Upstate New York on a ski trip. She was loading some skis up onto the top of a car when a drunk driver came careening down the snow-thickened road. And just like that, in a snap of the fingers, his car barreled toward her, smashing her between two cars and crushing her legs.

Rebecca was taken by ambulance to the nearest hospital but had to be life-flighted to New York. She was in a coma for days. She was in the hospital for a year. Her daily conversations became a constant plea not to amputate. After numerous surgeries, she was told she could keep her legs, but the scarring and damage would be permanent. The pain drew out. An incident—a tiny,

tiny moment—created a lifelong result. Her beautiful, delicate legs, her dancing limbs, weren't ever the same. It was devastating.

The natural human response to a tragic event like this is anger and sadness. Confusion and disbelief. And inevitably all those feelings can boil over and trickle into a longer-lasting feeling of self-pity. Never-ending frustration. Deep despair. A victim mentality. I mean, wouldn't you feel sorry for a beautiful young woman, sitting in a wheelchair being forced to give up her life's dream?

But Rebecca never has and never will be a victim. Her spirit is all about overcoming fate, not succumbing to it. Rebecca knew feeling sorry for herself would be normal. Her self-pity would be understandable and completely valid. But she also knew feeling that way would do nothing to improve life's condition. It would only lengthen and deepen the pain.

No matter where you are, no matter what has happened, life can only move in two directions as it could for Rebecca: better or worse. It does not matter how tragic or impossible the situation you find yourself in seems. You can choose to linger in the pain, or you can choose to move forward and make a wonderful life out of what you have. It's all about your belief systems. We can't change the circumstance, only our reaction to it. I can hear my friend Robin's voice in my head as I write that.

"React differently," she'd tell me. And I'd ask, "How do I do that, Robin?" And she'd say, "Lisa, chose it."

The Dalai Lama XIV once wrote, "There is a saying in Tibetan, 'Tragedy should be utilized as a source of strength.' No matter what sort of difficulties, how painful experience is, if we lose our hope, that's our real disaster."

Rebecca didn't lose her hope. She didn't pity herself. She didn't think of her life as ruined or her possibilities as stunted. She chose to see the potential in the space she'd been given.

Within three years of her accident, Rebecca started a company where, instead of dancing, she employed dancers. She took the knowledge she had and the love that she had and started doing event and party planning. Her philosophy was: I can still be the best at what I do, even if it wasn't what I thought I would be doing. *My life can be better than I originally expected.*

Her business flourished immediately and she's now one of the top party and entertainment planners in New York. She owns Just Rebecca in Hicksville Long Island, New York, and creates fantasies for people. Not just parties. Her clientele is a long list of celebrities, high-powered individuals, and those who saved every penny to have a birthday, wedding or celebration of a lifetime. She understands what people need from a night like that and the memories they need to be left with. We could name drop here and blow your mind a little, but that's not her style. She protects the identity of her clients the same way she holds a secret.

"If I 'what if' myself to death," Rebecca says, "I'm going to spiral downhill and one day wake up and find myself in sweat pants and 700 pounds. I'm going to go from bad to worse instead of bad to better. What if the drunk driver had come down the road thirty minutes later? What if he hadn't had a drink that day? What if I hadn't gone on the trip at all? What if I'd stayed on the slopes a little longer? What if, what if, what if. It's so easy to pity yourself. The 'what if's are endless. But they're pointless, too. This is my situation. This is my reality. I own it and now have to make something of my life. There is no questioning that what happened is terrible. But what's the point of dwelling on that? It's what happens now; it's what I do with the future that matters."

Rebecca's left leg should have been amputated. She shouldn't have walked again. That was the doctor's verdict. *Never.* But something deep inside her said, "I'm not going to be in a wheelchair my whole life. I'm not going to go through life sitting down."

And so she didn't.

Instead of falling into the "Why me?" trap, she decided to say,

"Why not me?" In the hospital she told her friends and family, "As soon as I get out of here, I'm getting some white cowboy boots." She was going to trade in her high heels for something that fit her better. She was going to find something new to love. Today we could probably buy an island if we sell Rebecca's boot collection; it's so much of her identity!

Despite what the doctors said, Rebecca can walk now. She can run. She can ride a bike. Snowshoe. Ski. Go boating. She gets up on her beautiful legs, admittedly not as good as they were before, and makes use of them. In our early twenties I was working, going to school, and taking coaching class after coaching class. But she would call me and say, "Don't tell me you're tired and going to sleep. We're dancing until the clubs close because I can." Rebecca influenced my drive and my energy. Our friendship is one of the strongest bonds in my life, and she will never hear me say, "I'm tired and my feet hurt."

"I do the best I can with the capabilities I have" Rebecca says, "The thing is, I know it happened, and it's terrible that it happened, but it can't be the only thing every single day. Life's too precious to center it on your misfortune and the reason I am so strong-willed and successful is because there's a part of each one of my friends in me...My friendships are invaluable."

Products of Our Beliefs

Maybe, like Rebecca, you've had an event so big and so devastating that you feel as though your dreams and ambitions were shattered in one full swoop. Or maybe it's not one given event, but rather a succession of life circumstances that make you doubt your potential, causing you to question yourself and hesitate. Big or small, no matter. Somehow you've let life convince you that what you wanted was too much. You weren't cut out for your dreams. It won't happen.

Too often we're led to believe that the LOT we've been cast dictates who we become. That we're a product only of our environments. But that couldn't be farther from the truth. It's not what happens that matters; it's how we react.

Consider the story of two boys growing up in the slums in poverty. They're surrounded by drugs and violence. They aren't looked after by their parents. No one misses them at the dinner table. There isn't a dinner table. Their time is their own. One boy filters into the standard crowd—what's expected of a boy in those parts—and starts running drugs. He stops going to school. He doesn't care. What does an education matter? He's never getting out of there. And no one cares enough to set him straight. The other boy goes to the park. Every day he's at the basketball court, shooting for hours. He gets a job outside of the neighborhood, walking two miles each way to be a stock boy at a grocery store. He tries to stay out of the fray, keep his head down, keep going. He stays in school, even if the school isn't that great, because he's got a feeling that it still matters.

And it does.

Because he stays in school, because he keeps practicing, he gets a scholarship to play college ball. And then there he is at a young seventeen-years-old with a full ride to a great school where he can study to be a businessman, while the other boy is still standing on the street corner.

Out of one situation, one environment, come two futures. Both are possible, but what actually happens depends entirely on the boy's response to his environment.

We've been conditioned to believe that the world is so small. That there's only so much we should reasonably expect of our time on earth. People put us in boxes and stereotypes claiming that our possibilities are dictated by who our parents were, where we were born, what our skin color is, how pretty we are, how much money we have. These sweeping statements oversimplify the situation. They create a belief culture where people focus more on who they're expected to be rather than who they want to be. And that's the real problem. Because once you crack open the door and let these restrictive beliefs in, they have the tendency to become self-fulfilling prophecies.

You start saying things like, "I probably won't get the

scholarship, so I shouldn't even apply," or "No one from my family has ever started a business, why should I be any different?" And just like that, you close your own door. You've listened to others preconceived notions rather than listening to your own, and you're no better for it. You've become a product of someone else's beliefs.

If Rebecca had listened to hers she would have been classified as "disabled" and would constantly think, "This is as good as it gets." Is she handicapped? Why don't you ask her? She would say the handicapped are those who can do so much with their life but choose a small game. They're the takers. The ones who sit back and wait for someone else to do something.

Think about it this way. You have a small garden outside in your backyard. It's just a small plot of dirt. In it you plant some flowers, some little seedlings that have the potential to bloom. But, as with most gardens, weeds creep in. They start to encroach on your flowers' growing space. You have a couple of options. You can either let the weeds remain, killing off your flowers and littering your garden space, or you can weed them out. You can remove the junk and cultivate a space where your flowers can bloom.

Creating a healthy belief system is much like that. While it would be great if we went through life with only positive people and situations around us, that just isn't possible for anyone. Life is real and it can be hard. You'll come across people who doubt you and will want to hold you back. You'll have discouraging events happen that will make you second-guess yourself and your ambitions. But all of these negative people and events are weeds. You need to remove them or you'll never be able to see your dreams bloom.

Society's limitations are only prophetic if you give them credence. If you expand your worldview and foster a belief culture that goes against the grain, you've already exponentially increased your chances of success. Beliefs have a remarkable capacity to transcend any situation. If you believe, and I mean really believe in yourself, you open up entirely new doors that the world says you shouldn't have access to. But if you let your environment dictate your future, you're reinforcing your own glass ceiling. You will only go so far and so high.

What you have to remember is: It's not up to them; it's up to you.

Perseverance

The biggest roadblock in creating a healthy belief culture is overcoming adversity and failure. Defeat can be demoralizing. It can turn hope into doubt in the blink of an eye. And it's so easy to get sucked into the helplessness of it all. It's much easier to say, "I can't do this," instead of getting back up and trying again. But it's how we deal with hardship that truly determines our trajectory in life.

The key to being successful is transforming your definition of failure. So many of us see failure as permanent, an event that we can never remedy, but that's not the case. Failure is not a final event. It is a pit stop on the road, a lesson that can teach you how to better navigate the future.

I think about Rebecca all the time and how she manages, each day, to overcome her adversity and make her handicap an asset. She doesn't see her accident as a hardship that must blemish everything. Instead, she focuses on the good, on what she can control. Instead of being angry, she says, "I am the sum of what has happened to me. I am only able to be where I am today thanks to what has come before." What was a tragedy has now allowed her to start a thriving business she never would have created. And she's thankful for her life.

"I'm very happy," she tells me all the time. "I do everything I ever wanted to do."

How did she do it? And how does she continue to do it? Perseverance. Because every single day, in small but important ways, she improves herself. She believed that she would have a successful life no matter what and backed that belief up with hearty action.

No, it didn't happen overnight. It took time; it took

determination. But never once did she go backward. She was always moving forward, even if it was inch by inch.

If you indulge in your pain and pity, you strip yourself of your personal control and your ability to do something about your situation. You enable a false feeling of helplessness, and instead of standing on solid ground, you resign yourself to quicksand, constantly being engulfed further and further in negative beliefs.

But is there ever a situation—no matter how bad—where you really can't do anything? Where you can't decide to chin up and move forward, even if it's little by little?

It took over thirty years and 400,000 people to build the pyramids—all without the power of modern machines. Greatness rarely appears overnight. It is far more about the determination and wherewithal than it is about the quick flawless, sprint.

In *Awaken the Giant Within,* Anthony Robbins writes, "Many of our country's greatest achievers have succeeded in spite of running into huge problems and barriers. The difference between them and those who give up revolves around their beliefs about the permanence, or lack thereof, of their problems. Achievers rarely, if ever, see a problem as permanent, while those who fail see even the smallest problems as permanent.

Once you adopt the belief that there's nothing you can do to change something, simply because nothing you've done up until now has changed it, you start to take a pernicious poison into your system."

You cannot get you want by hanging up your hat. The only permanent thing you can afford to have in your life is perseverance.

Creating Your Belief Culture

You are here reading this book because you want to make a change, because somewhere deep inside you believe, quite simply, that where you are is not where you're supposed to be.

And you're right. You were created for more. You were created for a better life.

But whether you have it is up to you.

In order to move forward, in order to have a breakthrough, you're going to have to revolutionize your beliefs. You're going to have to set aside your doubts, weed out the negatives, stop making excuses, and cultivate a healthy belief system that can thrive in both hardship and health.

Stop listening to the culture that tries to hold you back. Stop trusting the negative and doubting the positive. Remember always that it's your actions not the conditions of your life that matter most.

Will you be your own glass ceiling or will you accept and fully embrace that—no matter what happens—there's more out there for you than what you're settling for?

CHAPTER 4
Do What Lights You Up

"Be so good they can't ignore you."

—Steve Martin

Here we are at the crux of it. Do what you love. We've heard that phrase a million times. It sounds so simple, so obvious, that we don't really catch it for what it is: bad advice.

What's that? You say. I shouldn't do what I love?

Well, in a way, no you shouldn't. But before you have a panic attack, let's back up. I'm not asking you to resign yourself to a life of paper pushing and boredom. I would never do that to you. To get the life you want, I'm asking you to be intentional rather than indulgent.

That's a big concept, so let's unpack it.

Think about all the things you love to do. One of my friends, for instance, loves to cook. She could spend all day in the kitchen, making meals for the people she cares about. She gets lost in the recipes. She finds it therapeutic. And while she's a good cook, she's not a great cook, so making a living putting food on the table could be tough. And while she loves it now when she's doing it for the satisfaction of serving people she holds dear, she might not love it so much when the pressure is on and the old money ladies start squawking in her ear that the chicken is dry. Cooking is what she loves, but cooking is not what she should do. It's what I like to call a "get to" not a "have to."

A few years back, author Penelope Trunk wrote something I absolutely love: "I am a writer, but I love sex more than I love writing. And I am not getting paid for sex. In fact, as you might imagine, my sex life is really tanking right now. But I don't sit up at night thinking, should I do writing or sex? Because career decisions are not decisions about 'what do I love most?' Career decisions are about what kind of life do I want to set up for myself?"

Are light bulbs going off yet? Penelope hits the nail on the head there.

We've got to be honest. This is real life, not fantasyland, so we have to have an awareness of ourselves and of the world in everything we pursue. Having a strong sense of awareness does not mean being small-minded or overly practical. Instead, awareness gives us the tools we need to best navigate our surroundings and scale that mountain. You wouldn't go attack an enemy in the battlefield without first studying their strengths and weaknesses, would you? Exactly. So why not do the same for yourself?

Realistically, there are plenty of things that we love to do that either we (a) can't really make a living doing (champion Nerf gun fighter, anyone?), or (b) might love, but aren't quite good enough to pursue as a means of income (like my friend who loves to cook). There's also the very realistic chance that while we might be able to do what we love for a living, the pressure of having to earn an income off our first passion can suck the joy right out of it. I've seen that happen so many times.

If we insist on only doing what we love for a living, it can be shockingly detrimental to our life's potential.

Take the example of Steve Jobs. As author Cal Newport points out, if he'd done what he loved, he would have spent his life as a Zen teacher, walking around barefoot. But clearly, that would have missed the boat of his true and full potential.

Here's an alarming truth: if you're willing to stop this endless quest of "doing what you love," I guarantee you'll find yourself much happier, much more fulfilled, and much more successful. Find what it is that you are good at and use it as the *vehicle* so you can "get to" do what you love most.

How? Let's break this down a little bit further.

If you haven't before, I want you to stop what you're doing now and take a personality test, like the Myers-Briggs. There's a short version which makes it super easy and leaves you with no excuses not to do it. Once you've done that, I want you to whip out your journal and write down the answers to the following questions:

1. What are your strengths?

2. What do you absolutely hate doing?

3. What are your personality traits?

4. What activities do you find yourself engaged in when doing them? In other words, what keeps you from checking your watch?

Then, I want you to make a list of ten jobs that are good fits for your strengths and personality traits and that will keep you engaged. Exclude any job that requires you to do something you absolutely hate. For instance, if you hate sitting in a cubicle from 8:00-5:00, scratch off the office jobs. There are plenty of careers where you can be on your feet and active, or at least where you don't have to be in a chair all day long.

Now, I want you to make this list regardless of (a) your training; or (b) the public's perception of said careers.

Why?

Firstly, because you can always get the training and become qualified to do a job.

And secondly, because it's not the public's life you're living; it's your own. So who cares what they think?

To echo Penelope's point, finding the right job is about creating the life *you* want for yourself. And maybe the life you want isn't the life everyone else wants. And that's okay! In fact, that's wonderful.

Taking this test, answering these questions, it's all about learning to do what you are rather than doing what you love. That's a good phrase isn't it? It's coined by Paul and Barbara Tieger who wrote a book of the same name: *Do What You Are*. That's what Steve Jobs did. And that's what I did, too.

Years ago I remember hearing someone say, "You can have it all . . . just not all at the same time." I didn't listen. I fell in love with network marketing because it allowed me to do what I love most: working from home, coaching, and raising my children. Had I listened to that advice, I would have put off either having kids or becoming a self-made millionaire. But since I never listen to advice I don't like, I did both—and at the same time! You can, too!

How, you ask? Well, I'm an extrovert. I love helping people. I love speaking and getting in the trenches and being active. So being a life coach and network marketer is such an absolute perfect fit. Maybe I didn't spend my whole childhood dreaming of this career like so many girls dream about being things like models or beauty queens. But I do what I am. Every day I utilize my strengths. And that gives me passion and satisfaction. And that's the ironic thing, isn't it? If you do what you are, you'll often find you end up loving what you do because you are being true to your natural self.

Over the years, I've discovered that the art of getting what you want is all grounded in intentional living. You have to be perceptive and self-aware to capitalize on your time, your strengths, and your energies. You have to visualize the end, knowing where you want to go, if you want to have a chance of getting there. And this all boils down to spending the time necessary to figure out who you are and what lights you up. You have to do more than what you love. You have to do what you are. So what are you waiting for?

Reflection Questions:

1. Did you take the Myers-Briggs test? How does your current career path line up with your results?

2. Can your current job get you where you want to go?

3. Do you think "do what you love" is good advice or bad advice? Why or why not?

4. Could there be alternative careers you haven't considered that would be a good fit for your strengths and personality type? Take time to brainstorm a few. Be willing to think crazy outside the box.

5. Would you be willing to make a big shift in your career? Why or why not?

6. How could thinking intentionally about your personality traits and strengths help you identify a more fulfilling career path than the one you have now?

7. Giving up doing what you love for a living doesn't mean you have to give up doing what you love in general. How can you continue to keep the things you love as high on your priority list?

CHAPTER 5
Visualize the End

*"A clear and focused mind will last a lifetime.
Getting your mind in shape is nothing less than
the key to sustainable success in the world."*

—Russell Simmons

Our planet is populated with bodies that are just always so busy. People who move and move and move, whipping up dust, causing a big commotion. But what are they creating? Sometimes we get so caught up in the movement, we lose sight of what should be our anchors: purpose and destination.

The art of getting what you want begins in knowing what you want. And who you are. And we're not playing the small game here. Sure, you want a long vacation, a bigger house, more money, more time. But we're talking big vision, big life-scale. What do you really want for your life? If you were to cast your reel five years into the future, what would you hope to pull back? Ten years? The end of the road? What is the legacy you are creating? Who will read your eulogy and what will they say about you?

STOP, and reread those questions. Who are you really and what is it that you desire? And just for fun, imagine you can have it all. Where does your mind go?

So often we fall into the trap of waiting for some specific achievement to fulfill us. A person, a job, a vacation. You name it. But instead of filling us up, these surface goals often leave us tired, worn out, lonely, and searching to fill a void. They're short-sighted; they can't possibly satisfy what we must satisfy on our own.

Visualizing the end is about choosing to live intentionally with a strong perception of the final target. Only in understanding where you want to go can you make wise choices about how to live on a daily basis. When you don't have a set goal or ambition of the bigger sense, you're shooting blind. And while you might be busy, that doesn't necessarily equate to being effective. It just means your time is ticking away.

It is remarkably common to get swept away by the busyness of life. You climb ladders, not because you want to ascend them, but because they're there. You go out to dinner with people not because you enjoy their company, but because they asked. Continually, you fill up your plate because you don't like the look of it empty.

But have you ever considered this?

The man who sits at home on the couch each day watching reruns on TV, is nearly as close to achieving his dreams as the man who runs around all day, taking meetings and shaking hands without any set objective. If you don't know what you're trying to accomplish, if you don't understand what is deeply important to you, your busyness is just that: busyness. Only when you really tap into and understand the large passions of your life, can you manage the day-to-day with purpose and conviction.

Your time is a devotion. And each moment you spend doing one thing, you can't spend it doing something else. It is far better to stop now and determine what you want for your life—even if that makes you temporarily feel like you're "falling behind"— than it is to continue rushing ahead, hoping you'll run into your purpose. Or, even worse, thinking you know what you want for your life without ever giving it any sincere consideration.

How often do you hear about people who make quick, impulse choices and then go on to regret them? Buying a dream car, but not checking out the mechanics. Saying "I do," without ever discussing the real core topics. Or how about the people who choose a career path because it's what someone else wanted for them? Or accepting the first offer that comes their way? How often does that work out well? How often is that the best choice?

If you're not willing to be thoughtful with your choices, you are severely limiting your potential in life. Whether you want to or not, you will most certainly direct your efforts and your time into hollow victories rather than meaningful ones.

Stephen Covey once wrote, "People find themselves achieving victories that are empty, successes that have come at the expense of things they suddenly realize were far more valuable to them. People from every walk of life—doctors, academicians, actors, politicians, business professionals, athletes, and plumbers— often struggle to achieve a higher income, more recognition or a certain degree of professional competence, only to find that their drive to achieve their goal blinded them to the things that really mattered most and now are gone."

Or consider the wisdom of Malcolm Muggeridge: "When I look back on my life nowadays, which I sometimes do, what strikes me most forcibly about it is that what seemed at the time most significant and seductive, seems now most futile and absurd."

It is easy to be under the influence of the moment. It is captivating, it is emotional, it is *now!* But present pleasure is a fickle master and it is not a wise one. It is the man who eats all his summer harvest, but stores nothing away for winter. That is no way to survive and certainly no way to thrive. Instant gratification is destroying our culture.

My friend Cathy is an amazing example of visualizing the end. She graduated from Boston College in 1985 and interned in a hospital studying sports medicine. And while she loved it, she knew from an early age that she wanted to work for herself. So with that big-picture knowledge, she charged forward with her own business of aerobics and personal training. She grew to coach major athletes and fitness experts, getting her own show on MTV. She's pioneered a niche in the fitness industry where she coaches both men and women in sport-specific training, nutrition, stage presentation, choreography, and careers in the fitness world, founding Cathy Savage Fitness.

For Cathy, she says its essential to understand that the present is a process. "You have to recognize that you need wisdom, you need trial and error, and you have to constantly be trying for more. When things don't go your way, you have to choose to be a doer rather than a victim. It is about seeing the long-term and realizing the constant room for improvement, rather than getting focused on small-item present issues. You have to make a declaration about your life, then own up to it."

Cathy lives each day with intention and self-awareness. Although busy, she is not chaotic. She is generous with her compliments, her listening, her praise, and her encouragement. She has the time to tune in and be grateful for the meaningful relationships in her life. People want to be around her because she is grounded and focused. She isn't searching; she understands the journey and is fulfilled. Cathy knows what is deeply important to her and she uses those bits of knowledge as guideposts in her decision-making. While she lives in the present and creates short-term goals, she's wise enough to make every movement with a constant understanding of her destination. She is so successful in everything she pursues because she begins with the end in mind.

The question is: do you?

Reflection Questions:

1. What big-picture goals do you have for your life?

2. Break your goals out into segments. What would you like your life to be like in 5 years? 10 years? At the end of the road?

3. Do you find yourself intentionally making choices to achieve these goals?

4. What lifestyle do the decisions you make each day reinforce?

5. Do you identify with the bodies who are busy doing a lot of nothing?

6. What busyness can you cut out of your life to be more effective?

7. How do you think beginning with the end in mind would change the landscape of your life?

CHAPTER 6
Wear Your Blinders

"Great spirits have always encountered violent opposition from mediocre minds."

—Albert Einstein

You hear these stories now, all the time, of young people who are conquering the world. You hear about how fifteen-year-olds are inventing computer programs and making technological advances that will radically change the way we communicate and live. You hear about child prodigies who became landmarks in their field before they were even out of diapers—children who have done more by the time they've reached high school than most of us have done in the past three decades.

Matt Mullenweg was a nineteen-year-old freshman at the University of Houston when he created WordPress—an open source blogging tool and content management system used by more than 17 percent of all websites in the world.

Kim Ung-yong—the individual with the highest IQ on the planet—entered university as a physics student at the age of three, when most of us were finger-painting and sucking down graham crackers. At age seven, he was invited by NASA to study in the United States.

David Karp launched Tumblr in 2007, at the age of twenty. He sold it to Yahoo! in May of 2013 for $1.1 billion.

It doesn't seem like such impressive success should be discouraging. It should make us excited and thrilled—*look at the world's potential!* And yet, if we're really being honest, watching others flourish so quickly, so easily, well it can be disheartening. Why? Because as Theodore Roosevelt wisely noted: *comparison is the thief of joy.*

More often than not, when you hear about somebody else's success, your own flaws become remarkably pronounced. You see what they have and what you don't. You put your life under a microscope and hone in on your 'weaknesses.' You realize you're no longer in the body of a fifteen-year-old. You have wrinkles and some gray hair. You have a mortgage and kids and responsibilities. You have baggage—things that appear to get in the way.

And because of this, you whisper lies to yourself like, "I'm too old," or "My time has passed," or "I don't have the luxury of time and money like they do." You lament to yourself that you can't do what they did.

But these thoughts, these comparisons, they're just excuses. They open a window of doubt so you can elegantly bow out of the race. You look at the world and say: *I would, but . . .* and then you list all of the "valid" reasons why you're going to stay right where you are, why you're going to give up on your dream.

What you hate to admit is that there are only two real reasons people give up on the life they want: fear and laziness.

The truth is, you were right. You can't do what they did. But that's not because who you are isn't enough. It's because you weren't born David Karp or Kim Ung-yong or Matt Mullenweg. You were born as you, to do the things that you were uniquely created to do, when you were uniquely created to do them. You can't be anyone else half as well as you can be yourself. So why bother trying? Wouldn't it be far better to be the most successful version of the only person you can be: you?

And here's a remarkable thought: they can't do what you can. Only you can fill your spot in the world.

Here's what you need to start repeating to yourself every day, every hour: My time is now. I am strong mentally and physically. I am ready to take this on. I have all that I need. I will begin now. I will continue to trust the process even when it scares me. I will stay focused on the outcome and the results. I will attract people who guide me.

Right now, no matter where you stand, you have everything you need to succeed. If you truly decide and commit to something, there is practically nothing you can't do. And remember: you can't fail unless you quit. Fear of failure is the easy phrase for lazy people. It keeps them from getting started and leaves them stuck in the land of complacency. They're the type of people who buy into the term impossible. But I don't believe in impossible. I believe there's just a person that hasn't yet figured out how to do what they're looking to do. So go. Try. Do. Succeed!

And that's the scary part isn't it? Not that you *can't* succeed, but that you *can*. That you have the power to leave the average life you're living and claim a new one where you refuse to settle for what is easy and comfortable and second best. The fact that it's never too late creates a remarkable amount of responsibility. Just a minute ago, you could bow out of here gracefully. But now, well, now you have potential. You have enough at your disposal this very second to start living the life you've wanted to.

Marianne Williamson never spoke truer words when she said, "Our deepest fear is not that we are inadequate. Our deepest fear is that we are powerful beyond measure. It is our light, not our darkness that most frightens us. We ask ourselves, 'Who am I to be brilliant, gorgeous, talented, fabulous?' Actually, who are you *not* to be?"

I have a friend who was climbing the corporate ladder. Just in her late-twenties, she was shooting up it at a remarkable speed, promoted to an executive position. She was attracted by the title and the money and the security. But no sooner had she accepted the promotion when she realized she was climbing the wrong ladder. This was not the life she wanted. She was working long hours for people she didn't respect, doing tasks she didn't enjoy. There was no fulfillment. But how could she quit? This is what so many people spent their entire lives working toward. And she already had it at so young an age!

What my friend realized then though is that even if it were everyone else's dream in the entire world, it was not her own. It was not what she was created for. And the only reason she would stay in the job was because it was comfortable, it was secure, and, when it came to worldly appearances, it looked like the right thing. But those are never good reasons to continue doing something. Knowing this, one day she took a big, long deep breath and, without so much as a next job lined up, she resigned.

"At some point," she said, "if you're going to get the life you want, you have to do an about-face. You have to rid yourself of the unhealthy activities and people who are standing in your way. You have to make really scary, faith-filled choices. You have to turn off the world's noise and leap."

What we so often forget to acknowledge about the remarkable stories of the likes of Matt Mullenweg and David Karp are that those stories are outliers. That is not the precedent for success. More often than not, history tells us that victory comes in the middle to later years of life where you have tried and failed and then tried again. Or, like my friend, you have gone stridently down a path until, quite abruptly, you come up against a life-changing moment that forever makes your destiny clear.

Very few people are born geniuses. Very few people get it right the first time. Everyone, on the other hand, is born with the ability to commit, be persistent, and hunker down for the long haul. You can be successful on your own terms.

Don't believe me?

Consider Winston Churchill, who failed the sixth grade. In every public office he ever ran for, he was defeated. But then, at age sixty-two, he became prime minister. Or how about Steven Spielberg who applied for film school at the University of Southern California three times and was rejected at every single go. And Marilyn Monroe who saw her first contract with Columbia Pictures run out because the executives believed she wasn't pretty enough or talented enough to be a star. She went on to become one of America's most notable sex symbols.

These icons couldn't have succeeded if they kept focusing on others around them who seemed to be sky rocketing ahead. Instead they put their blinders on and kept plucking away, believing in their own potential and doing what they loved.

Just as important, these people didn't abide by naysayers—the people who told them they'd never be good enough. The world is populated with opinionated people. And while there are some select individuals who might rally and be your cheerleader, it's far more likely that you'll come across the opposite—individuals who will willingly and eagerly tell you that you're not good enough, that your idea is too crazy, that your dream is too big. These people will try to squash you into the status quo because the status quo is what they're comfortable with. And because you are human and susceptible, it's easy to start believing what they say, taking their words as fact rather than fiction.

But naysayers are not truth speakers. They are just people with poor opinions and small visions.

In his book, *Think and Grow Rich*, Napolean Hill wrote, "Opinions are the cheapest commodities on earth. Everyone has a flock of opinions ready to be wished upon anyone who will accept them. If you are influenced by 'opinions' when you reach DECISIONS, you will not succeed in any undertaking."

What he means is this: you must decide for yourself what you are worth and what you can achieve. And you must believe in that wholeheartedly. If you let the opinions of others plant seeds of doubt in your mind, you're already a goner. You cannot succeed when you're burdened by a watered-down view of your potential. Instead, as much as possible, surround yourself by people who believe in the human capacity for greatness, who will cheer you on and help you get back up when you fall. Then, on a daily basis, remind yourself of the truth of your potential and the depth of your desire. Be rooted in that.

Doubt and faith have no business being in the same room. If there is one, the other cannot exist. If you succumb to the opinions of others, you will have given up your faith. But if you persist in your belief in yourself and if you're dedicated to your goal, doubt has no wiggle room to get through the door.

Consider Walt Disney, who did not start out a master of success and had numerous reasons to quit along the way. At a young age, he was fired by a newspaper editor because—and I quote—"he lacked imagination and had no good ideas." The first studio he founded in 1922, Laugh-O-Gram Studio, went bankrupt just a year after opening its doors. And in 1937, Disney was on the edge of bankruptcy again, only to be saved by the success of the release of *Snow White and the Seven Dwarfs*. During the creation of Disneyland, the proposed theme park was rejected by the city of Anaheim because the city believed it would attract low-rung folk. The opposition Disney ran up against time and again was small minds—people who could not see or believe the future he himself envisioned.

I know. It's not an easy fight, but it's an essential one. One of the biggest obstacles to success is the unhealthy influence of others. Because you're human, you compare yourself constantly with others, measuring up how much better or worse you're doing. You listen to people and take to heart their words of discouragement: *you can't do this, you're not prepared, you don't have it in you.* And those thoughts have the power to destroy you.

Stop listening to the racket.

In his book, *Ordering Your Private World*, Gordon MacDonald writes, "Few of us can fully appreciate the terrible conspiracy of noise there is about us, noise that denies us the silence and solitude we need for this cultivation of the inner garden."

When you get swept away by the world's noise, you miss your true calling and destiny. You focus too much on what other people are doing, thinking, and feeling at the expense of your own future. It's only by stepping back, turning off the public voice, and listening deeply to yourself that you can have the clarity and courage to move forward.

Never let anyone live in your head rent-free. Negative, toxic people are happy being "comfortably numb," so when you go out and create change, it makes them feel uncomfortable. It makes them feel guilty. They think, "She did it; I probably can, too." And they hate that thought because they were fine where they were. And now there you are, challenging them. So instead of supporting you, they criticize you.

Who cares? They are *not* going to pay your bills.

You will be amazed at how toxic people will slip out of your life and new souls will begin to appear. Coincidence? Doubt it. I believe in the Law of Attraction. You will manifest whatever it is you declare and think about.

I tell everyone there are two hard and fast rules to live by when it comes to the influence of others, and I will share those with you now:

1. Create your own destiny by doing the action steps necessary to have that result. BEGINNING NOW.

2. When people offer you "advice," take what you need to help move you forward and leave the rest behind.

Write those down. Remember them. Live by them. Instead of focusing on the potentially negative influences around you, hone in and ask yourself the question that really matters: Is what you're doing and achieving giving you freedom and fulfillment? Are you staying true to what you believe?

If so, keep going.

Reflection Questions:

1. How do you feel when you hear about the success of your peers?

2. Is the success of others a motivator or a discouragement?

3. Are you using a factor of your life—such as age, money, location—as a crutch, enabling you to avoid the pursuit of your dreams?

4. Who are the most influential people in your life?

5. Do they speak words of encouragement and wisdom into your life or words of opposition?

6. What voice are you in the lives of others? Do you move people forward or hold them back?

7. What steps can you start taking today to weed out the negativity of others?

CHAPTER 7
Persevere

"Even if I knew that tomorrow the world would go to pieces, I would still plant my apple tree."
—Martin Luther

It was August 1999, and my friend Jan was going to Turkey with her children. Her husband, though American born, had Turkish parents, and Jan always thought it was important to steer clear of just a simple vanilla American upbringing. This other country round the world was a part of who they were. Her children should know it. Jan herself had gone a couple years before and thought the experience with her children would be wonderful. Thankfully, her husband's parents still had a summer home there, and so Jan packed up the kids and headed to Eastern Europe for a month.

Her children then were young, growing little things. The oldest was six, trailing down to the youngest at 10 months. They were just settling into their new life abroad when, a week into the trip, there was an earthquake. A large, monumental shaking of the earth. And all around, the house started to crumble. Not slowly, but in one swift move. Forty-five seconds after the start of the earthquake, Jan lost four of her children. The house fell down upon them.

Jan was caught in the rubble for twenty hours before being pulled out. One of her daughters, then only three and a half years old, also survived. She had been lying in a single, twin bed with her sister, their toes touching. Her sister didn't live, but she did. And that precious brave girl stayed alive after being buried in the rubble for thirty-six hours. She was stuck in a dark little hole, with no one to reassure her, no food to eat, no water to drink, no sense of safety and comfort. And then, a day and a half later, people she didn't know speaking a language she didn't understand, pulled her little body from the rubble and, eventually, to a face she knew: her mother's.

While her daughter had no injuries, Jan was severely hurt. There were numerous surgeries. There was paralysis in her arms. She couldn't move. For months after the earthquake, Jan couldn't do anything for herself. She couldn't bathe. She couldn't eat. She couldn't dress. For the longest time, she had to rely on others to do that for her. Due to the nerve damage, it took a year before she was able to regain function of her body and a year and a half until she was really back to normal.

While at the time it seemed impossible, Jan now looks back on the time of stillness as a mercy:

> *It allowed me to grieve instead of busying myself*
> *so completely that I could smother the emotions*
> *that came with what happened and who I lost. I*
> *had no option but to sit and be fully aware of my*
> *situation.*

It was the most difficult position a human could be in, one of complete emotional destruction. But Jan knew that even though they were gone, she was still here. No matter how much it hurt, she still had a life she had to live. And while she could grieve continually and never get back up on the horse again, so to speak, that would not be a life that would honor her children. So Jan asked herself: what's the most meaningful thing I can pour my life into?

Even before Jan had her first child, she knew she had a heart to be a mother. It was built into her genes. And so months after the accident, after many spilt tears and long conversations, Jan and her husband decided to adopt. The children they had lost had been so unique and individual. Those hearts could not be replaced ever. But Jan and her husband figured just as they had lost children, many children had lost parents. It would be a blessing to be able to give someone a home.

The earthquake happened in August, and in March of the next year they began the adoption process. They believed adoption would take a few years. That's certainly what they'd heard. But in May, just two months after they applied, they got a call that there was a child for them in Kazakhstan. Jan and her husband flew overseas just a few weeks later and visited the orphanage. They had been planning on only adopting two children at most. But when they arrived and saw the conditions—children without diapers, the smells, the lack of love—they knew they needed to care for as many of the children as they could. And so they flew back home to America with four precious new children—three two-year-olds and one, one-year-old.

It has been nearly fifteen years since the earthquake, and Jan's family is knit together close, a completely unexpected and yet perfectly bonded group. Her oldest daughter, the one who survived the earthquake, is now seventeen. She has never had any nightmares, no post-traumatic stress. It's a blessing. Jan misses the children she lost every day, but she has new joy in her life that she never intended, and so she focuses her energies on the joy all of her children have given her over the years, rather than the sorrow that could so deeply wound.

"You tell yourself so many stories," Jan said, "so many lies. And when I was sitting there in my grief, literally paralyzed and unable to move away from it, I so often heard myself saying things like, 'My life is over,' and 'I'll never make it through this.' But you do make it through. And you can. Sure, it's hard. Sure it's painful. But you've got to believe good still exists. You have to use your mind to power through. There is beauty on the other side if you let yourself believe in it. I decided if I would dwell in my mind on the pieces of truth rather than the lies I could tell myself, I would survive. What you think about, you bring about. It's in our DNA."

There are so many answers inside each one of us. Stillness and a quiet mind allow the body and soul to process, purge, recreate, and move on. It is through the constant busyness that we get lost. When we don't allow the pain to surface, giving ourselves time and room to really grieve and confront a situation—like Jan did—we get stuck in a vicious cycle that often leads to more detrimental behaviors such as addiction, insomnia, infidelity, gossip, and self-destruction.

How many times have we heard of someone gaining or losing a considerable amount of weight when hardship happens? Or what about becoming addicted to prescription sedatives, drugs, or alcohol? Gossip? Infidelity? By numbing ourselves and trying to cover the pain, we stay in denial about what we actually need to deal with. Then we begin to shift the conversation away from the real issue—our feelings—and toward the new issues we've created.

But feelings buried alive never die, no matter how we try to mask them. In some insidious way they rear their ugly heads and lead us down a path of deep discontent. If you want to climb out of the hole rather than spiral down, you have to go through the middle of the issue. Go for it, cry about it, face it. Get help. But deal with it.

To me, Jan is an angel. Her story is the perfect picture of perseverance, showing us all how we can sit and be still so we can begin again.

There are obstacles in life that will throw you down and make you feel like never getting back up again. You will want to quit. You'll believe nothing at the end of the rainbow could be worth this amount of pain and effort.

But when you get in this situation, ask yourself these questions:

1. Where am I?

2. Do I like it here?

3. Do I want to stay?

4. Is there a better destination?

If you find that where you are is a place of pain and heartache, get up. Choose to power through. Because where you are is not where you're intended to be. You have to set aside your title of "victim" or "martyr"—even though those titles in themselves can give you comfort—and you have to start owning the title of "overcomer." It is not easy to be an overcomer. It is a challenge you have to daily put your mind to. Again and again, you have to choose to move past your circumstance.

The life of a victim is not a fruitful one. It is a painful one and a sad one. But the life of the overcomer is filled not only with challenge, but also with joy and thanksgiving. It's up to you what title you choose to wear.

Reflection Questions:

1. What resonates with you most about Jan's story?

2. Take out your journal and write about a situation where you lost something important to you. How did you react?

3. Does this situation still affect you today? How?

4. Consider a situation in your life where you

persevered. Was it worth it?

5. What is a circumstance in your life now where you're choosing the title of "victim," but need to start owning the title of "overcomer"?

CHAPTER 8
Say No

"And it comes from saying no to 1,000 things to make sure we don't get on the wrong track or try to do too much. We're always thinking about new markets we could enter, but it's only by saying no that you can concentrate on the things that are really important."

—Steve Jobs

It's time to buck the age of the "yes" person. You know who I'm talking about. The one who says yes to every opportunity that crosses his/her path. The person who checks "joyfully attend" on each invitation, goes to seven cocktail hours a week, makes an appearance at every event. As a culture, we've had it hammered into our heads for so long that we should never turn down an opportunity because we never know what might come of it. And that's all well and good. In theory.

But being a "yes" person is exhausting. And not only is it exhausting, it's actually detrimental. It stretches you so thin that there's no part of your life you can focus on and bulk up.

So why do we do it? Whether you realize it or not, there's a "reward" for every choice you make. And if you're a yes person, you keep choosing to overextend yourself—becoming drained physically, emotionally, and financially—for a reason, even if that reason is as simple as it makes you feel validated with others. Your over-extended lifestyle can allow you to play hero—*Look how unselfish I am, helping so many people!*—or victim—*Poor me, I never have time for myself because I am there for everyone else*—or martyr—*I have to do everything for everyone, or the job will never get done right.* And those titles—hero, victim, martyr—they make you feel good and special and worthy. They are the benefit that causes you to keep doing what you're doing. But if you no longer want to be stretched so thin in your life, dabbling at everything and mastering nothing, you're going to have to give up your hero, victim, and martyr mentalities, and change your behavior.

Dr. Nancy Elder is an assistant professor at the University of Cincinnati's College of Medicine. In *Primer Magazine*, Elder was quoted as saying, "Like everything in life, any time you take anything to an extreme—either you say 'yes' to everything or 'no' to everything—you're going to be in a position that's often untenable and often unhealthy."

Think about it this way. There are two women, both having ten people over for dinner. One of the women tries to play the hero and victim: she leads a Girl Scout meeting in the afternoon, drops off the dry cleaning, lets out and feeds the neighbor's dog who's on vacation, then gets back in time to clean her house for dinner. She doesn't actually have time to cook, so she grabs a couple of bottles of wine and some take out. It works, but it's not what she was hoping for when she invited everyone over. "Sorry," she tells them. "I would have made something more special if I didn't have to run around town doing X, Y, and Z all day."

The other woman chose not to make so many commitments that day. Instead, she knew she wanted to put together an intimate party with delicious food for her guests, so she set the day aside entirely to go to the store, cook, and set her table. Both women were able to have their dinner party, but only one was able to have the party she wanted. Why? Because she knew doing everything would jeopardize the quality of the one thing that really mattered to her. One woman played the hero and the victim. The other woman decided to not worry about the titles, and simply focus on what mattered.

Anthony Robbins, one of the greatest thinkers on personal fulfillment and success, says, "One reason so few of us achieve what we truly want is that we never direct our focus; we never concentrate our power . . . In fact, I believe most people fail in life simply because they major in minor things."

Get it?

The point here is not to become a "no" person, but to realize that learning to say no effectively is really about allowing yourself to achieve your goals.

When people consider what they want to do with their lives, they often focus on the two pieces of bread and no filling. Here's what I mean by that. On the starting side, you begin with a list of goals and dreams. On the end side, you have a list of desired results and achievements. What you often don't have is the middle—the filling.

In between discovering who you want to be and actually getting there, you have to make a number of choices. You'll be presented with various opportunities, and you have to navigate those with grace and assertiveness. Sure, you can say yes to everything that comes your way, but then your path is haphazard, long, and truly impractical. Sure, you can say no to everything, believing you have already planned the path perfectly yourself, but that's remarkably limiting and small minded.

If you want to achieve anything, you need to master the great balancing act of being intentional with your yes's and no's. Don't just hand them out. Recognize opportunity vs. distraction. Recognize doing something out of unnecessary obligation vs. doing something because you know it's the right thing to do.

Learn what you want. Learn what is good for you. And follow after that with a fearless boldness.

Consider your body. It knows what it needs. You can fill it with alcohol and sugar, tons of starches, but it won't be happy with you in the morning. It will have a physical and negative reaction to the choices you made. On the other hand, if you feed it what is healthy for it, what helps it function the way it was created to function, you will have more energy, more stamina. You will have an improved life.

"The most important thing that people who [say yes or no] do well is to temporize," Elder said. "It's important to acknowledge the request. 'Yes I hear you asking this. Yes I hear you asking to put this on my plate,' then saying, 'Give me twenty-four hours to think about this.'"

I have a friend named Shane who made a pretty difficult, but pivotal choice in his life. He grew up having an incredibly strong family. His mom was a stay-at-home mom and his dad was a successful dentist. He was the oldest of four kids, a very determined spirit. In July of 1995, it was the summer between Shane's freshman and sophomore year of college. He was home for a few months and had been out one evening with his family. At 11:30 on that particular night, a drunk driver came speeding down the road at 100 miles per hour and slammed into Shane's car with his entire family inside: his three brothers, his sister, his mom, and his dad.

Shane doesn't remember much of the accident. He has just flashes of memory. But people told him later what happened. He woke up abruptly with the car on fire, and he got up and began pulling his entire family out. He went on autopilot, saving the people he loved. His mom was wedged between the floorboard and the engine block. No one could pull the car off around her. But somehow, as the car grew further engulfed in flames, Shane was able to free her and pull her to safety.

Shane came out of the accident unscathed. His siblings suffered minor injuries. His mother had a crushed face and a crushed tailbone. But his dad didn't make it; he passed away at the scene.

The loss of Shane's dad was an incredibly significant moment in his life. Shane had been his father's son. He had been studying pre-med at school with the intention of going to dental school after graduation. He wanted to open a dentistry practice with his dad. Right before the accident, they'd just passed that beautiful threshold between a father-son relationship and a bond of good friends.

For the next few years after his father's death, Shane continued down the pre-med path, but something inside him was feeling unsettled. His heart simply wasn't in it. He began to realize he had been living his father's dream and not his own. He had wanted to share a special bond with him, but he was pursuing that at the expense of what he really loved.

Shane remembered his dad always telling him, "Whatever

you do in life, make sure you love it from when you get up to when you go to bed."

Dentistry was not that. So Shane listened deeply to his desires and callings. He learned to be intentional with his yes and his no, and he decided not to pursue the career of dentistry out of an unnecessary obligation. His next years took him down an entirely different route. He started pursuing exercise physiology and worked as a personal trainer. It was a natural fit and he had untold success. Today he trains some of the world's top professional athletes.

Shane could have remained a victim. He could have become a dentist and spent his whole life feeling unfulfilled, by telling people: I'm doing this because it's what my dad wanted me to do. Instead, Shane was willing to say 'no' to his dad's vision, and 'yes' to his own. And ultimately, his willingness to make that choice fulfilled his dad's wishes for him far more as Shane is able to wake up each morning and go to sleep each night knowing that he spends his days doing what he loves.

Maybe for you, what you need to say no to isn't as big as an entire career shift. Maybe the incident that sparks your change won't be as significant an eye opening as Shane's was. But listen to yourself. Refine your purpose and determine what you need to weed out in order to achieve your goals.

Maybe you need to remove the people and personalities in

your life who drain you and steer you down the wrong road. Maybe you need to say no to some of your extracurricular activities so you can have more time and energy to focus on what really matters. Maybe you need to say no to your eating habits, and instead choose a healthier approach to life that will give you more energy and strength. We have so many opportunities to become better people who are living more intentional lives.

The real question is: what are you willing to give up in order to have what you don't have?

Reflection Questions:

1. Consider the decisions you make on a given day. Are they intentional? Are they supporting the goals you want?

2. Are you a "yes" person or a "no" person?

3. Do you have a hard time saying no to people? Why?

4. What people, situations, or activities do you need to say no to but currently aren't?

5. What do you think it means to concentrate on your power?

6. If you were concentrating on your power, how would your days look different?

7. What are you willing to give up to achieve the life you want?

CHAPTER 9
Fail Beautifully

"There is only one thing that makes a dream impossible to achieve: the fear of failure."

—Paulo Coelho

Successful people fail. And they fail with frequency. They fail not because they're not good enough, but because they were brave enough to show up.

The motto of a low achiever is if you don't expect too much, you won't be disappointed. But you can't be who you want to be by remaining who you are.

If you really want to pursue your dream and make it a reality, you have to take ownership of your life and play an active role in the daily decision-making process. You have to expect a great deal of yourself and you have to be willing to fail. If you are not willing to fail, you will never succeed.

There's a plague running rampant through our society now. It's called complacency. People no longer take ownership of their lives. Instead, they adopt the "hands-off" approach to their futures, letting the chips fall where they may. Why? Because if they don't "own" their lives, they can pawn off their bad situations onto someone else. They can pass the blame. X didn't happen because of Y. A didn't work because of B. Sure, in the hands-off life you never fail. But you also never succeed. The best you'll ever be is mediocre.

Failure is one of the most misunderstood concepts in American culture. So often we see it as an end result. A negative. A blemish on our records. But failure is never an ending point. It's a result—a mere event on the way to the final destination. You either fail before you succeed, or you fail before you quit. But you never have to stop at failure.

What you really have to sink your teeth into is the understanding that failure is the only way you learn. It's the path to leadership. *That didn't work, let me try this.* Did you know that the acronym for fear is False Evidence Appearing Real. I love that because fear isn't something that happens to the weak man. It's something that happens repeatedly to the determined man. So embrace it as an awesome vehicle for learning, and stop enrolling other people in your drama about what didn't go perfectly the first time. If we're being honest (and aren't we always?), it's draining, and no one really wants to hear about it. If you quit after the first fumble and burden everyone with your self-pity, what kind of leader does that make you? Exactly. Failure keeps it real. It keeps you relatable. And if you power through it, it makes you awesome.

Heed the Wisdom of the Fallen Man

Whether you realize it or not, how you choose to confront failure will greatly determine your ability to succeed.

Most people are terrified of failure. They're terrified of being embarrassed by a bad idea. They're terrified of making the wrong choice. They're terrified of not doing things perfectly. They're terrified of having other people laugh at them. They're terrified of losing what they have—even if what they have isn't very good—because they're comfortable with the life they have.

You get the point. They're just plain terrified.

The fear of failure freezes people in their current lives. It stalls their ability to move forward, and leaves them driving continuously around a roundabout, never having enough courage to get on the real road.

But if you never risk having a bad experience how can you ever really have a good one?

In her beloved book *Bird by Bird*, Anne Lamott writes, "Perfectionism is the voice of the oppressor, the enemy of the people. It will keep you cramped and insane your whole life . . . I think perfectionism is based on the obsessive belief that if you run carefully enough, hitting each stepping-stone just right, you won't have to die. The truth is that you will die anyway and that a lot of people who aren't even looking at their feet are going to do a whole lot better than you, and have a lot more fun while they're doing it."

Have you ever met anyone like that? The perfectionist? The one who lives so carefully and quietly, who is so intent on making the right impression that they risk making no impression at all? These people, these perfectionists, they rarely put anything out into the world for fear that it will be ridiculed or laughed at. They spend their lives preparing rather than acting, talking rather than doing. They believe if they wait for the right time, if they work hard enough and are careful enough, they can remove the element of risk. They can take away all the potential pitfalls and do things perfectly, sans failure.

Perfectionists want the world to believe that they're so self-aware that they can do everything flawlessly if given the proper amount of time. But perfectionists aren't self-aware; they're self-absorbed. Perfection is inextricably associated with significance.

Perfectionists believe they are significant enough to be a matter of interest for all of society, and so they strive to be perfect because they don't want others to witness their guffaws. They think everyone is looking at them all the time, and they can't afford to mess up.

But here's a reality check: people are too busy with the junk in their own heads to dwell on you or me. The people around us aren't keeping a running tab of when we fail and when we succeed. They don't have their binoculars out waiting for the next pitfall. They're too occupied trying not to fall themselves. And frankly, if someone has the time to sit around, wait for me to mess up, and then laugh about it, really how valuable is their opinion? I'd always prefer to hear the opinion of a mover and shaker who spends their time failing and getting back up, rather than that of petty gossip who is so busy laughing at others that they don't take a good look at themselves.

One of my favorite poems is "The Guy in the Glass" by Peter "Dale" Winbrow, Sr. It puts the pursuit of perfection and the opinion of others in its proper place:

> *When you get what you want in your struggle for pelf*
> *And the world makes you King for a day,*
> *Then go to the mirror and look at yourself*

And see what that guy has to say.

For it isn't your father or mother or wife
Who judgment upon you must pass.
The fellow whose verdict counts most in your life
Is the guy staring back from the glass.

He's the fellow to please-never mind all the rest,
For he's with you clear up to the end.
And you've passed your most dangerous, difficult test
If the guy in the glass is your friend.

You may be like Jack Horner and "chisel" a plum
And think you're a wonderful guy.
But the man in the glass says you're only a bum
If you can't look him straight in the eye.

You may fool the whole world down the pathway of years
And get pats on the back as you pass.
But your final reward will be heartache and tears
If you've cheated the guy in the glass.

I don't care what lies you've been telling yourself, let's say this loud and clear for the record: It's impossible to do things perfectly. *Perfection does not exist!* No matter who you are, there will always be someone smarter, prettier, more talented. There will always be a better time and a better place. That's not a bad roll of the dice; that's reality. So stop trying to meet everyone else's expectations by putting on a show. Instead, take a look at the man in the glass. Are your actions ones you can be proud of?

It's the people who have bad experiences—but who dare to have experiences—who succeed far more often than those who choose to have no experiences at all. Failure is the greatest teacher. It shows us our missteps. It unveils our weaknesses. It sharpens our strengths. Our failures show us what our successes never could: how to be better.

I dare to say that no one in a position of success has arrived there unblemished by the long road to the top. When they look in the mirror, they probably see a lot of scars. But they're proud of them. Everyone doesn't do it perfectly the first time. Or often the second time. I certainly didn't. The road is riddled with setbacks and letdowns and mounting frustrations. But that's a glorious provision.

Next time you try and you fail—because there certainly will be a next time—instead of shying away from future efforts, I challenge you to take a lesson from Robinson back in Chapter 2 and interpret your situation differently. Listen to your failures. Become close with your disappointments. Take the heartbeats of your letdowns. In paying close attention to what went wrong and why, in choosing to learn rather than mourn or pity yourself, you're being heartily equipped to get back up and travel much closer to your desired goal.

Have you ever heard Sara Blakely? At age twenty-nine, she didn't look like someone to invest in. She'd failed the LSAT, was hawking, of all things, fax machines, and had roughly $5,000 in her bank account.

But she knew there was something special about her—that one day she'd be doing something amazing if she just kept at it. Sara had the most impressive emotional stamina. She had a gut feeling about herself that she wouldn't let go of, no matter what other people said. When she was twenty years old, she took a mental snapshot of where she saw herself in the future and knew some day, some way, she'd be on the *Oprah Winfrey Show* talking about what she'd done with her life.

Fast-forward nine years from her "snapshot moment," and Sara was twenty-nine. She was headed out to a party for the night and wanted to feel a little slimmer, so she cut the feet off of her control top pantyhose in order to wear them under her white pants. It was a much more flattering and comfortable look, and it dawned on her then that this was something women could actually use.

She read a slew of books on trademarks, burning the midnight oil at Georgia Tech Library after work each day, learning the ins and outs of pantyhose patents. She took her concept to numerous attorneys hoping to get their help in the patent process, but most thought she was off her rocker and sent her packing out the door. So Sara wrote the patent herself. It was approved, and she trademarked the name SPANX online.

With the patent intact, she began shopping the idea around to a number of manufacturers in North Carolina to help her construct a sample product. According to Sara, every mill owner she approached asked the same three questions: "And you are? And you are representing? And you are financially backed by?" The answer to all three questions, of course, was Sara Blakely. She was doing it all on her own.

Most owners returned her earnest query with a quick no. She was a "nobody," she didn't have any connections, and she had no investors. To them, it seemed like an obvious pass. But Sara had something no outside investor could guess the value of: she had courage.

From a young age, her dad taught her to fail big. Each day he'd ask her, "So, what did you fail at today?" And according to Sara, if there were no failures he'd be disappointed. Why? Because failure is not a final outcome. It's one result. It's a pit stop on the road to success. You just have to be determined enough to take the whole drive.

Sara's dad taught her that failing meant you could see what you'd done wrong, what you'd done right, and how you could do it better the next time. Failing was never a bad thing; it was celebrated.

So unlike most people, the "no's" didn't stop Sara. They kept her going. She didn't give up and, inevitably, luck with a manufacturer struck when he took the product idea home and told his daughters about it. And the girls, Sara's ideal consumers, saw something in the product the slew of businessmen didn't see. They called it what it was—brilliant—and then and there Spanx was born.

Today Sara owns 100 percent of the company. She never took one outside investor. And Spanx is now estimated to have annual sales of $250 million and very big profit margins. Not too shabby.

In an interview with Kathy Caprino at *Forbes*, Sara said her single most important piece of advice for aspiring entrepreneurs is this: "Believe in your idea, trust your instincts, and don't be afraid to fail. It took me two years from the time I had the idea for Spanx until the time I had a product in hand ready to sell into stores. I must have heard the word "no" a thousand times. If you believe in your idea 100%, don't let anyone stop you! Not being afraid to fail is a key part of the success of Spanx."

Don't Stop Short

When you stop letting your fear of failure rule you, there's still more work to do. You also have to develop a solid determination like Sara did. The sad truth is most people give up right before they're about to achieve success, right on the one-yard line. They choose to quit rather than power through. Can you imagine if Sara had stopped sharing her product idea with manufacturers just before she met the factory owner with two daughters? What a tragedy that would have been. She'd probably still be selling fax machines!

Have you heard the iconic story of the gold rush? A man in California was determined to strike it rich. He spent months upon months prospecting for gold in the hills. He found pockets of gold here and there, but never anything substantial. Eventually he grew tired of the process and decided that his fortune wouldn't be found there. It was fruitless. So he sold his land and his tools to a new prospector and moved on.

The new gold prospector was a smart guy. He hired people who understood the land: an engineer, a geologist, and a land surveyor. Together they determined the best places to dig and went to work. With just a little effort, the new prospector struck the goldmine—only three feet from where the previous owner had stopped.

If you want to succeed, you have to have a long-term, big-picture focus. Our culture is saturated with overnight success stories that teach us if it doesn't happen quickly, it won't happen at all. We hear about these overnight sensations and, like the pictures of the skinny, airbrushed models in the magazines, we're taught that's the norm.

What a load. The norm is not for victory to happen with a flick of the fingers.

Do you know what I get asked all the time? What the shortcut is. People want to know how to make a million dollars tomorrow. They want to have 20,000 Facebook friends in thirty minutes. They want to create a brand with credibility in a week. But they don't really want to do any work. And they certainly don't want to fail.

A very few people in this world will get lucky. They'll get it right the first time. They'll become famous at lightning speed. And good for them. But it does you no good to rely on being the overnight sensation. Instead, expect to be here for the long haul. Expect to work for it. Expect to fall flat on your face, and expect to be in for a big education. Because failing big is learning big. And that's what makes you better.

A low achiever gives up when they get a little dirt on their knees and a little embarrassed blush on their cheeks. They stop three feet short of gold. But the real deal keeps digging, even when they're tired, even when they've failed a thousand times.

As Thomas Edison so graciously put it, "I have not failed 10,000 times. I have not failed once. I have succeeded in proving that those 10,000 ways will not work. When I have eliminated the ways that will not work, I will find the way that will work."

And find it he did.

The question is: in a society of instant gratification and quick fixes, are you willing to pay the real price for success? Are you willing to sweat it out? Are you willing to fail 10,000 times, and give up what you have to have what you don't? If you really want to achieve something big, you have to make the necessary sacrifices on a daily basis and embrace those sacrifices until you stop saying, "I have to do this," and start saying, "I get to do this!" What a monumental shift.

Right now, you are either taking steps closer to your goal or you're moving further away from it. Everything counts and everything matters. But here's the part I love: *At any moment you can recommit and choose to shift.* So, go for it now! Tomorrow isn't real. There is no guarantee you have it. You're acting with significance and entitlement when you assume that tomorrow is yours. So stay here and work from *this place*. This is a wonderful place to change the conversation. It's time to start saying, "How can I?" rather than "What if . . ."

Reflection Questions:

1. How do you define failure?

2. How do you believe failure can have a positive impact on your life?

3. Write about a time you've failed and taken it hard. How did you act? If you chose to interpret the failure differently, how could things moving forward have been better?

4. How does the fear of failure impact your daily decisions?

5. What would you do differently about your life if failure weren't an option?

6. What did you get most out of Sara's story?

7. Is there something you've quit pursuing that you shouldn't have let go of?

8. Have you ever stopped three feet short of gold?

9. What does success mean to you?

10. What you are willing to give up to have what you don't?

11. What would happen if you did "fail"? Is that enough to keep you from trying?

I BELIEVE IN YOU! It's not about success or failure. It's about how you arrange the story in your head.

CHAPTER 10
Renew, Renew, Renew

"Better keep yourself clean and bright. You are the window through which you must see the world."

—George Bernard Shaw

Have you ever heard the Old Indian proverb that says, "Everyone is a house with four rooms, a physical, a mental, an emotional, and a spiritual"? Author Rumer Godden says that "most of us tend to live in one room most of the time but, unless we go into every room every day, even if only to keep it aired, we are not a complete person."

The bulk of this book has been about equipping yourself for success—expanding your worldview, raising your standards, overcoming the fear of failure, and learning to be decisive. But a key part of getting what you want is also self-love and making sure you keep yourself healthy in all areas of your life—physically, mentally, emotionally, and spiritually. If you're not tending to your well-being, it won't take long for you to burnout.

It's so easy to neglect our multiple "rooms." Most of us do as Rumer suggests and spend all our time hanging out in one space. We focus so heavily on one area of our lives to the detriment of the others, and very few people realize how interconnected all of our "rooms" are.

I know what you're thinking. This is a bunch of new age hokos pokos. The emotional body? What does that even mean?

But no matter how it sounds, you have to take care of yourself—your whole self—if you want to have a shot at success. Everything about your body is intertwined, so if you're not caring for your emotional and spiritual portions, if you're not exercising your mental muscles, your physical body suffers as a result. Each one of your rooms needs nourishment and tending to.

I have a friend, Billy, who is a personal trainer and all-natural body builder in New Jersey. He tells me all the time that it isn't about getting somebody in the gym, kicking their ass for an hour, and making them look like a walking washboard. It's about making their total life better. To him, if he just addressed the physical body, he'd be doing them an injustice.

One of his first clients was a thirty-nine-year-old woman just coming out of a divorce. She had no self-esteem. She'd come into the gym all buttoned up, none of her skin showing. She was covered head to toe, completely ashamed of herself. But within ten months, with complete determination, she'd lost forty-two pounds. The best part, though, was when she came in one day and told Billy she wanted to do a body building show. He was so thrilled because it wasn't just that she was looking healthy again, it was that this woman who, less than a year prior wouldn't show a piece of skin, finally had the confidence to step up on a stage in a bikini.

Later on Billy trained a woman who was in her mid-fifties. She was in an ultimate low in her life. She had two special needs children, was extremely overweight, and, to top it all off, she had bulging discs in her back. When she came into Billy's facility, she couldn't walk the length of a football field without being in agonizing pain. She told Billy how one day she tried to walk down the boardwalk, but couldn't even make it half way before falling to the ground in agony. Her husband had to go get the car to bring her back home.

Every time she would go to the gym, Billy would start by asking her how she was feeling. The emotional connection was a key part of his physical betterment plan. Within a year, she'd shed sixty-four pounds. She went from a size 16 to a size 4. Her bulging discs were practically back to normal. She was able to get her life back and enjoy the luxury of really being on her feet.

And why? Because she made a point of renewing her health in every "room." And she found that when she was feeling better emotionally, she was better equipped to work harder physically. And when she could look in the mirror and be proud of herself, she was stronger emotionally. Through Billy's training, she learned the power of her entire body and the beauty of full health.

There's a book called *Love Yourself Like Your Life Depends on It*. It's by Kamal Ravikant—a guy who was a Silicon Valley entrepreneur who hit the lowest of the lows. He spiraled down into a deep sickness where his body entirely broke down. He was dealing with failure, both financially and relationally. And the emotional burnout was literally killing his physical body.

Eventually he pulled himself out of it and came through to the other side much stronger because he bought into the seemingly simple, but powerful philosophy: I love myself. He repeated those words to himself frequently. All day, every day. And they had healing powers, not only for his heart, which had fractured and broken, but for his physical body that had been so badly weakened.

"Think about it," he told his friend, the author of *Choose Yourself*, James Altucher. "When someone is in love, they almost magically look better. I needed to be in love with myself to feel better. So much of what had happened had weighed on me until I collapsed. Now I needed to love myself. It became a mantra for me."

Create Time for Yourself

A large part of loving yourself is not just bettering who you are, but really allowing yourself time to rest and renew. Inhale and exhale. Go ahead, let out a deep sigh. Again.

We live in a busy culture. People are constantly moving, scheduling appointments, going from A to B. People equate spare time and rest with a waste of time. *Doesn't every minute need to be packed to the brim in order to be successful?* The world says, *Won't we fall behind if we're not going, going, going?* Or, even worse, by the time some of us sit down to relax, read a book, watch a show, or just breathe, we fall asleep! We're exhausted running the rat race.

One of the biggest lies society tells us is that a busy person is a successful person. But the two aren't necessarily related. A busy person fills their time while a successful person is intentional with their time. Those are two very different approaches.

Consider this scenario. Two men get in their cars. One man knows where he's going and drives thirty minutes and arrives at his destination safely. The other man jumps in his car and is constantly being distracted and taken off route. He drives for eight hours and ends up no closer to his destination, his day wasted by errands that cost him both time and money. When he goes to bed that night, he can't even remember what he was trying to accomplish when the day started. One man was busier, but he definitely wasn't the most successful one of the two.

Rest and rejuvenation are so critical because they allow us to exchange the scattered busyness the second man experienced for a sound mind like the first man possessed. Rest, in its infinite peace, gives us three core benefits:

1. **Rest gives you clarity.** When you're busy, it's as though your mind gets overtaken with weeds. It becomes so cluttered and hectic that you can't possibly parcel through and separate what's important vs. what is simply taking up space. You stop striving for a specific goal, doing tasks that will lead you to that goal, and instead simply start striving to get through the day. Successful people don't get anywhere by shooting blind. They know and heed their target. When you allow yourself to rest, the clutter dissipates. You have clarity about what's important to you.

2. **Rest allows you to develop your purpose.** Once you have clarity about what's important to you, you can start fleshing out a plan of action. Your days can become intentional and full rather than scattered and busy, actively working toward getting the life you want.

3. **Rest allows you to be decisive.** When your mind is clear and rested and your purpose is developed, you are better equipped to stay on course. You're able to say "no" to the distractions and have the energy to say "yes" to the tasks and obligations that benefit you.

Continually Look For the Good

As you move forward and work to renew all the "rooms" of your body and create time for rest, there is one thing you can do for your health that will help beyond anything else: decide on happiness.

Do you remember Robinson? His mom shared with me a story, which is likely the best image I can leave you with. There was an old woman who was ninety-two-years-old. Her husband of seventy years had recently passed away and she was moving into a nursing home, as it was no longer sensible for her to be on her own.

When she arrived at the nursing home, she looked as she always did, clean and made-up. Well-dressed and prepared for the day. She sat in the lobby and waited to be shown to her new room. It took a number of hours for them to finish readying, and finally a kind nurse, middle-aged, came into the lobby to get her and show her to her new home. As they walked to the elevator, the nurse described the contents of the room, including the eyelet curtains fluttering across the windows.

"I love it!" the old woman exclaimed.

The nurse patted the woman on the back reassuringly and said, "You haven't even seen it yet. Just wait."

For so many years, the nurse had led old men and women through the facilities. Most grumpy and unhappy to be leaving their homes behind. But this old woman was different. And she said something the nurse never would have expected.

"That does not have anything to do with it," the woman said. "Happiness is something you decide on ahead of time. Whether I like my room or not, does not depend on how the furniture is arranged. It is how I arrange my mind. I have already decided to love it. It is a decision I make every morning when I wake up. I have a choice. I can spend the day in bed recounting the difficulty I have with the part of my body that no longer works, or I can get out of bed and be thankful for the ones that do work.

Each day is a gift, and as long as my eyes are open, I will focus on the new day and all of the happy memories I have stored away—just for this time in my life."

Reflection Questions:

1. What room do you spend the most time in?

2. What room is most neglected?

3. Take out your journal and name at least one way you can spend time in every room, every day.

4. What do you think when you look in the mirror?

5. Do you love yourself?

6. How could your self-perception alter your ability to lead the life you want?

7. Would you consider yourself a busy person or an intentional person?

8. In your journal, write out three times in your life where you tend to slip into busyness rather than intentional living. What can do you to make sure this doesn't happen in the future?

9. How often do you take time to rest?

10. What do you believe the personal benefits are for rest?

11. How can you realistically carve out time in your schedule to renew?

12. Do you believe people can decide to be happy?

13. What can you learn from the old woman in the nursing home?

ACKNOWLEDGEMENTS

Thank you to Mom for *constantly* being there for my children and me and always telling me to reach above and beyond. My friends, Michelle, Danielle, and Rebecca, who have been there every second of every day. My assistant, Monica, who gets it done. Jan, Billy, Shane, Rebecca, Cathy, Robinson... the people who contributed through their honesty and their vulnerability. Thank you for sharing your stories. And thank you Sheila McKenna for the awesome hair and make-up and Brian McAward for the cover shot. To David Dunham, at Dunham Books—if it weren't for you forcing the execution of this book, it would surely still be on hold. Thank you for your persistence and your faith in me and in this project. Thank you to Megan Byrd— you were a joy to work with and made the writing of this book a cake-walk. My brothers, Joe and Steve, and sister, Marie, who love and laugh abundantly. My amazing friends, team, mentors and clients and especially to my Dad, who made me believe I was special. I miss you, Daddy, and I secretly believed you.

ABOUT THE AUTHOR

Lisa DeMayo is a self-made multi-millionaire. She is also a certified life, executive and leadership coach with more than twenty years of coaching experience, and a top-level network marketer, recognized as one of the top income earners with Isagenix. She is also a member of the National Speaker's Association.

Lisa lives in New Jersey with her three lovely children.

To learn more about Lisa's workshops, seminars and speaking engagements or to receive her monthly letter visit her website: www.lisademayo.com, or email her at coachlisa@lisademayo.com.